MORE INCOME WITH LESS STRESS

Maximum Synergy Marketing,
Sales and Leadership

Dave Hershman

THE
HERSHMAN
GROUP
Finance ◆ Education ◆ Consulting

Library of Congress Cataloging-in-Publications Data

Hershman, Dave
More income with less stress: maximum synergy marketing, sales and leadership / Dave Hershman
p. cm.
ISBN 0-9710346-0-5
1. Marketing Synergy.   2. Sales Skills.   3. Leadership.
3. Customer Service
I. Title   II. Hershman, Dave
LCCN 2001089513

ISBN 0-9710346-0-5

Contributions by Bill Cates and Lynne Waymon are reprinted by permission of the authors. Edited by D.J. Mash.

Hershman Group books are available at special quantity discounts to use as premiums, sales promotions or in training programs. For more information, you may email the Hershman Group at success@hershmangroup.com or visit on the web www.originationpro.com or call 1/800-581-5678.

TABLE OF CONTENTS

INTRODUCTION

*"I like the dreams of the future better
than the history of the past."*
Thomas Jefferson

In today's world we have witnessed an incredible amount of innovation designed to improve our effectiveness in the business world. Twenty years ago it took several minutes to fax one page to another office. Today, we can instantly communicate with thousands of employees and customers—simultaneously. We have the Internet, e-commerce, cell phones, PDAs, broadcast faxes and email. Shouldn't we have extra time and less stress in our everyday lives?

All these technological innovations have brought us to a world economy that changes at the speed of the Internet. It has not given us extra time or less stress. I can remember vividly a radio talk show in October of the year 2000—the first year of the new century. The subject of this discussion? What are we going to do with our extra hour this year during daylight savings time!

We have more stress and less time in our lives because there are more possibilities than ever for our actions and what we can accomplish. If we can reach the world markets instantaneously, the possibilities are endless. Our competitors are now worldwide and they can reach our customers instantaneously.

The rules of maximum synergy are designed to help us accomplish more in less time with less resources—whether marketing or selling a product, managing employees or servicing customers.

A typical marketing book would offer 30 or more ways to market. But it is hard enough to find time to market one new idea, let alone thirty? All this would do is add additional stress to your life because you would now be aware of 30 more ways to market that you don't have time to implement.

Woody Allen says that ninety percent of life is just showing up. We say that life is not just showing up, but what you do when you get there. Every day millions of business people take actions that are just not effective because they don't have the time to effectively implement the same. Maximum synergy is designed to help you take your present actions and make them more effective.

Maximum synergy is designed to have you open your eyes a little wider to the opportunities around you. Soon you will see that you do not have to add additional marketing or management actions. You will see synergy partners and more effective tools at your fingertips. When you slow down you will see opportunities you have been missing for years.

We illustrate how maximum synergy brings less stress again and again by following the introduction of the rules with a treatment of a multitude of business topics from the development of a comprehensive marketing plan to management and customer service tools. We show how each of these topics can be made more effective through the use of synergy. Maximum synergy is demonstrated to have maximum impact when we highlight areas usually thought of in terms of operations and customer service (such as surveys) and show that they are really opportunities to increase your business.

We also indicate what traits each individual must have in order to effect these rules. Quite simply, you cannot implement any actions effectively without a great attitude.

On the other hand, if you believe that synergy will work you will be amazed at how simple it is to achieve more results with the same actions. The only way to *increase your income with less stress* is through limiting your actions, not increasing them. Good luck!

CHAPTER ONE
The Seven Rules of Maximum Synergy

"Make yourself necessary to somebody."
Ralph Waldo Emerson

The scientific definition states:

Synergism: "Joint action of discrete individual agents in which the total effect is greater than the sum of their individual effects"

Are your actions made up of many individual activities that are more effective than the sum of each activity? In other words, does each action build upon another? It is the seven rules of maximum synergy that are designed to help us produce more with less time and stress.

While classic marketing and sales literature tells us that we must spend additional time devising, revising and testing our solutions, in the real world we may get one shot at seeing whether these solutions will work. Each action must be as effective as possible because it may be our only shot. Our maximum synergy rules are designed to actually save time for those faced with the daunting task of implementing activities with too little time or other resources.

The following concept introduced by Stephen Covey, in *The Seven Habits of Highly Effective People* (Simon & Schuster, 1989), is borrowed from the scientific definition—

Two actions will bring a result of three or greater.

For those in business, you may ask, if I barely have the time to implement one activity how can I orchestrate the implementation of two to achieve maximum effects?

3

So we must advance a new, more realistic definition of synergy:

One action will bring a result of two or greater.

Of course, a definition does not bring us a result. If it was that easy to formulate two results through every activity, wouldn't everyone be doing it presently? It is through the seven rules of maximum synergy that we will be able to advance solutions that can bring results for everyone involved with the marketing or selling of a product or service or managing employees doing the same. Whether you are a part of an international sales force of thousands or an owner of a small business, these rules are designed to help open your eyes a little wider. When we move to the elements of a marketing plan—from the development of goals to the evaluation of results—it is only through the implementation of these rules that we will be able to bring the elements of the plan closer to reality in a world that demands immediate gratification of our efforts. In other words, it is not the need for the existence of goals that is important—but how we can more effectively achieve our goals.

Maximum synergy rule number one: every activity you undertake must achieve two results

Every activity has the potential for additional benefits. In the process of opening our eyes a little wider, we are able to identify additional results from activities we are undertaking every day. None of your activities take place in a vacuum. Sometimes additional effects are achieved but unrecognized because we are not looking. At other times, additional effects are not achieved because the activity is implemented too narrowly. Still other times, actions have negative effects upon our efforts and there is no recognition of these effects because we don't have our eyes open wide enough. Some of these every day actions involve incredibly simple activities such as driving cars and operating fax machines.

Nothing is more simple or common than our use of voice mail systems. Today we all have voice mails for individuals and companies. Voice mail is a great technology and can save time, but it can also work as a negative impact on sales. I have worked with banks that are constantly attempting to contact their present customers through the mail to cross-sell services from credit cards to retirement plans. Yet, when their customers call in to the institution on their own they are diverted to a computer to handle their transactions, completely obviating cross-selling opportunities that would be more cost effective for the bank as compared to their customer outreach efforts.

This brings us to the point of voice mails and synergy. Let's move to the level of individuals and voice mail. As an author, speaker and consultant with a national clientele I have had the pleasure of conducting business exclusively over the phone for the past few years. This method of selling holds true for many businesses—from telemarketing operations to national sales forces. For those who conduct business over the phone, playing voice mail tag can be quite frustrating and amusing.

When calling a potential client, there is now an 80 percent or greater chance that you or I will wind up in their voice mail system. There is also an 80 percent or greater chance that the voice mail will sound something like this:

> *"You have reached _____'s desk. I am on the other line or away from my desk right now. If you will leave a message after the beep, I will get right back to you."*

Of course, when your clients call you they are also likely to hear this very same voice mail message. As a matter of fact, the very first time a client is likely to hear your voice is on their voice mail or on your voice mail message. It is a basic fact, proven again and again through surveys, that clients are more likely to make a purchase because they like to do business with a certain individual. It is also a fact that they form a basic opinion as to this individual during the first seconds of initial contact. This is why we spend so much time trying to make a "great first impression."

Yet, most of the time what they hear is the above voice mail message. Great first impression, right? What you are basically telling your potential prospects is that they should call a few more people and hope for the best.

Why not use the message to tell them something about yourself or your product that will indicate to the caller that they have contacted the right person, instead of telling them what to do after the beep? As a matter of fact, if they don't know what to do after the beep, I am not sure that you want to do business with them! You can be assured that your clients do not care whether you are in the bathroom or on the other line because from their perspective you are not available to talk to them right there and then. The point is—everyone utilizes voice mail systems today. Why not leave a message that will help you sell what you are trying to sell—or provide a better level of service?

Of course, the key is being able to pinpoint a value-packed presentation without making your voice-mail too long. You basically have two short sentences to make an impact. We will talk about this concept at length later as we delve into the concept of "uniqueness."

Moving from voice mail, you can see that the first rule of synergy may apply to many aspects of your everyday business life. In my speaking business, I included customer endorsements and a speaking calendar on my fax cover sheets. This let my prospects know when I would be in their town and available. Do you make full use of your everyday activities, including travel time? Remember, the goal of synergy is not to add activities, but make better use of the activities you are already undertaking.

Maximum synergy rule number two: if you are marketing by yourself, you are wasting synergy

If someone asked me why I was successful when I was a salesman on the street selling mortgages 20 years ago (yes, I was 12 years old at the time), the answer was easy. It was because of the level of service that I provided. Merely ten years later, the secret of achieving major sales success would have evolved to the concept of value. Not that great service was not important—but now it was recognized that you must provide a certain level of value to your clients. What about achieving success in the Year 2000 and beyond? Now you must move to another level—one of partnership with your clients. Neil Rackham, in his industry leading work, *Getting Partnering Right* (Rackham, Friedman, and Ruff; McGraw-Hill, 1996), helps us evolve from the concept of added value to the trend in partnerships as he has studied major business relationships evolving over the years.

Rackham focused upon major partnerships between the companies who sell and those who purchase and utilize their wares. His focus is not upon two companies selling to the same target though he does cite a few examples of these types of partnerships. We can see examples of these types of partnerships everyday—credit card companies providing frequent flyer miles and real estate companies providing home warranties. It seems that everyone is interested in partnering to lower the costs of their marketing, finding additional sources of revenue or navigating an additional way into the hearts of their clients.

These concepts applying to large multi-national concerns also apply to small businesses and individual salespeople. Perhaps a car salesman cannot strike a frequent flyer deal individually but the car salesman has to recognize that there are others who are marketing their customers besides other car salesmen. Yours is not the only product that is purchased by your target. Once again, by opening your eyes a little wider you will find the perfect *synergy marketing partners*. If you are a sales manager you may be looking for the perfect synergy recruiting partners.

Who are the perfect synergy marketing partners? They have the same target market as you but sell a product that is related and non-competing. Even your competitors may become synergy partners if your clients and products are not completely mutual. This means that you must first clearly identify your targets and then become intimately knowledgeable regarding their consumption habits. Classic marketing training would tell us that we must know how our targets consume our own products—their purchase patterns are important as we plan additional marketing efforts towards our present customers. Maximum synergy production dictates that you must also know from whom your targets will purchase additional products on a regular basis. In many cases, this is not hard. If your customer purchases a car from you they are very likely to also need maintenance and body shop services some time in the future. Of course, most people do not envision needing a body shop—but when they do, the choice sometimes boils down to: fix the body or purchase a new car.

The basic question to ask about your synergy marketing partners: how can they benefit from your marketing efforts and how can you benefit from theirs? Why should you spend your resources (time and money) contacting customers and not achieve a second objective for another individual or company who could also include you within their marketing efforts? Sometimes these actions can be as easy as adding another flyer into your mailing (and vice-versa). Sometimes these actions might involve jointly calling upon targets in order to take advantage of previous relationships built up by the synergy partners. In other words, you introduce me to someone you know and I will introduce you to someone I know. In this case, the strength of your partner's relationships is essential to your success.

As your eyes open wider, you will find that anyone who is operating their marketing plan within a vacuum is not taking advantage of many synergy opportunities that revolve directly outside of their narrow field of vision. Why market alone when you can have many marketing with you? Synergy marketing partners must:

- ◆ be non-competitive;
- ◆ have the same general target audience as you;
- ◆ have a significant relationship with this audience; and,
- ◆ deliver value to their audience.

It is easy to see why a potential partner who does not have a strong relationship and does not deliver value to your target would not make an ideal partner. If they are attempting to deliver a product that is not thought of highly, you do not want to associate with their marketing efforts.

7

Maximum synergy rule number three: certain targets are more effective than others

Do you think that all targets are equal with regard to their potential effectiveness? You do not have time to market everyone in the universe, so your selection of the most effective targets will in large part determine the overall success of your efforts. Let me relate a personal experience that will illustrate this all-important concept.

After a long career as a mortgage producer and production executive, I found myself starting a business that would feature my books, newsletters and audio tapes as I traversed the nation speaking to companies—companies that of course would pay *big bucks* to hear me speak. Basically, I was in sales again and my product was me. Talk about needing a double sized ego: I not only had to have confidence that I was a great salesperson—but also that my product (me) was also great.

In theory, my first move should have been to begin calling upon major companies and associations within my specific target industry, the mortgage business. Who else was more likely to hire me than mortgage companies since I had published five books specific to that industry? My long-term goal of speaking within all industries would have to wait for now—I had to put bread on the table. Besides, target marketing is a much more efficient marketing strategy as opposed to trying to sell everyone in the world.

My most effective target within the mortgage industry would be large mortgage companies—perhaps the top 75 in the nation, as well as industry associations. Larger companies were more likely to have large sales/management forces for which they would need training and speaking services. Associations regularly have annual meetings for which they hire industry speakers. Including the divisions of the largest companies, this would amount to approximately 350 contacts. Now, it was time to start dialing for dollars . . .

What initially sounds like a targeted, effective approach turns out to be pretty widely scattered. My first question was—who is already calling on these companies? The answer to this question was simple—mortgage insurance companies constantly are competing for mortgage company business. I made the decision to focus on the five or six largest mortgage insurance companies (of which I had contacts because of my previous experience in the business). For one company the call was timely. They were trying to build their clientele within the central part of the country and sponsoring value-added training for their clients was where they wanted to go.

The result? Twenty paid speaking engagements through one initial phone call. Now I had account executives across the country personally visiting their accounts and speaking about a training program from Dave Hershman. This target was definitely more effective than making 300 or more phone calls to mortgage contacts directly. It would have taken at least 200 phone calls to generate the same level of business. By identifying a synergy marketing partner I was also observing synergy rule number two—I was not marketing alone. I should add one other item to this story—the mortgage insurance company also helped pay for the sessions. A full sales force selling and paying for my programs. Not bad with one phone call!

We are not talking about selecting a target audience. This is a much more specific exercise. Here we are talking about selecting the most effective contacts within your target audience. You are basically selecting your priorities. If you do not have enough time or money, it is doubtful you will have enough time or money to cover your entire target audience effectively. Therefore, use your precious resources to contact the targets that will yield the most effective results.

Maximum synergy rule number four: certain tools are more effective than others

The same concept applied to your target audience can be said for production tools. There are an infinite number of tools that can be utilized to increase business—from business cards to the Internet. One can never utilize all the tools at our disposal. We must make a choice as to which tools will be more effective to meet our objectives. Two points are very important to consider before we make a decision regarding this choice.

First, you do not have to invent a rocket ship to have an effective tool. Many tools are around us every day except we do not perceive them as tools. As a matter of fact, sometimes we think of these tools as obstacles. For example, we spoke about the potential uses of voice mail during our discussion of the first synergy rule. Like voice mail, the telephone and business cards are tools. *You* are a major tool. This is why we must have a discussion of "limiting factors" in this book—because without these limiting factors (attitude, honesty, etc), *you,* the tool, will be useless.

Second, tools must be integrated with each other. We cannot use tools independently of each other and expect to utilize the rules of synergy marketing. If we are running a newspaper advertisement, how will this relate to our use of a computer? If we are setting up a telemarketing campaign, how can our newsletter be integrated into this effort?

As we move on, we will be illustrating the concept of tool linkage as we introduce examples of effective tools throughout this book. For example, we spend a significant amount of time within the Networking Section talking about using one's sphere of influence, including the comparison of dealing with present customers versus cold calling. Public speaking is also introduced as a very effective tool for sales, especially as we fully utilize our synergy partners.

Maximum synergy rule number five: every action can be made more effective through additional doses of synergy

Adding synergy is akin to adding building blocks of effectiveness to your production efforts. No matter how good a newspaper advertisement, seminar, or direct mail piece is, we can make it more effective by linking additional goals, targets, tools and/or synergy partners. There is absolutely no exception to this rule. We may decide to halt our efforts because we have achieved our goals or have run out of associated resources to continue our efforts, but the potential will always be there.

For instance, perhaps you plan to deliver a gift to a client after a transaction is consummated. This is certainly a good idea—continuing to add value throughout your relationship. Let us say that the gift is flowers. We will assume that 99.9 percent of our customers consider flowers a valuable gift (excepting those who have major allergies). How could this action be made more effective?

First, you have already spent your most valuable resource (time) selecting, purchasing and delivering the gift. You have already spent your second most valuable resource (money) on the purchase. Why not involve a synergy partner? It takes absolutely no extra money or time to say that the flowers are from you and _____. If you are a car salesman, the flowers could be also from the insurance or finance company. If you are selling mortgages, the flowers could be from the real estate agent. Nothing is lost and something can be gained within the synergy relationship. Many times your synergy partner is a more effective target than your present customer. Synergy rule number one has been observed—a second objective from the same action.

Continuing with the same example, another way to add building blocks of synergy would be to open your eyes wider with regard to the transactions at hand. There are two transactions taking place here—one in which your customer purchases from you and another in which you are purchasing from your florist. Now, I have nothing against florists or flowers. I have been known to make a purchase from my local florist for special occasions—and not always because I was on the outs with "that special someone."

But the truth of the matter is—other than the flowers—what kind of value are you going to receive from the florist? You are certainly giving value to the florist, especially if you are making purchases on a consistent basis over the year. Why not purchase something from someone who can reciprocate this value? As a matter of fact, when you start searching for synergy partners you might find that the partner will donate a value package that will lower your cost of delivering the gift. And the synergy partner may very well deliver a package that is more valuable than flowers—especially if your target is a business. Flowers are nice, but a tool to help your business client produce more can be much more valuable.

What are the possibilities? Perhaps you are a real estate agent delivering flowers to the purchasers of a home at *the closing table*. Suppose you delivered a free consultation with a financial planner or a warranty on major appliances for 90 days. These gifts might be construed not as more valuable than flowers—but more on target for the transaction. In other words, the recipient is more likely to recognize the value. It is easy to see that a financial planner or a local warranty service shares the target with the real estate professional. Developing a reciprocal referral relationship from this juncture would be a natural step.

This brings us to the final point regarding building blocks of synergy. Adding building blocks gives us a mental picture of marketing activities that are connected with each other. They enable our actions to become diversified (dealing with different targets) and yet connected. It is not out of the ordinary for a business to implement a marketing plan that has separate and distinct marketing efforts. Perhaps the business might run a newspaper advertisement and in addition develop a telemarketing campaign.

It is easy to see why two marketing actions that are not connected would put us in a position to waste available resources. Implementing different actions depletes up our precious resources and has us looking narrowly in different directions rather than focusing within one area and taking a broader view. Focusing within one area uses much less of our resources and allows us to utilize those resources saved on synergy opportunities.

Maximum synergy rule number six: if there is no response mechanism, do not waste your resources

What is the goal of marketing? In speaking to thousands of salespeople and business owners each year, I often ask pointed questions such as: How many of you have published an article? For those who have raised their hands, I then ask what type of benefits they received from this marketing activity. Here are the typical answers I receive: visibility, credibility, free publicity, satisfaction and name identification.

Not that I am against free publicity or name identification. These are worthy goals. But we must remember synergy rule number one: two objectives for every action. I actually have published hundreds of articles in periodicals across the nation. Before you conclude that I spend every day writing an article you should note that I utilize synergy rule number five when publishing—building blocks of synergy. Each time I write an article, I find more places to publish the same. In other words, I might publish one article in ten different publications. When you take this approach it is not quite as hard to reach hundreds of publications.

Then one day I asked myself the same question—what am I trying to achieve? Yes, I was accomplishing something—but was it enough? I then decided to place a targeted response mechanism at the end of the article. The particular article was on the topic of telephone sales and was published in a major mortgage magazine. It should be also noted that I published the same article in a major magazine for public speakers (less than ten words had to be changed to reach this additional market).

At the end of the article I made a statement: If you call my 800-number you will receive a sheet that lists questions to ask people shopping price over the phone. At this juncture my phone rang off the hook and my staff reported receiving over 300 calls in less than one week. I could have implemented a *fax on demand* system so that everyone would have been able to receive the sheet automatically. Yet, this actually would have limited our exposure to the phone calls and our opportunity to sell additional products and services such as books and training. It is marketing activities that put us in front of our targets. But if the marketing efforts do not produce human interaction, there may be no opportunity to put our sales skills to work.

The bottom line is: I love visibility, but I can't eat it. I love name identification, but I can't eat it. The purpose of marketing is to increase our production. While an article can be a great vehicle for free publicity, if it doesn't make the phone ring you are wasting a major synergy opportunity. This concept is true for any type of marketing: direct mail, advertisements, radio, telemarketing and more. Offer something of value to your target and watch the phone ring! The newsletters I have offered to the mortgage industry for over ten years are guaranteed to make the phone of distributors ring because they use response mechanisms.

I have actually watched major companies such as banks send direct mail pieces with no response mechanisms (for example: *Take advantage of this great opportunity for credit card protection—now*). Instead, they have a telemarketing division disturbing people at home at dinner-time asking them to take advantage of the same great offer for credit card protection.

This is an example of two distinct marketing efforts that are not connected by synergy. Wouldn't the results be much better if the bank received phone calls from people who are at least interested in the topic? Perhaps a bank could offer a free special report on tips to protect one's valuables from fraud. The bank would lose a sales opportunity if they did not set up a system to talk directly with the respondents. Selling at the juncture in which our target's perception regarding the topic has been aroused is the most effective point of sale.

Maximum synergy rule number seven: if you are not offering something of value to your targets, why bother?

Your response mechanism must be something of value to all of your targets. Otherwise, your response mechanism will not produce the response necessary to achieve additional objectives. If your response mechanism is something that appeals to only a select few of the targets identified, you will be starting over again each time you attempt to undertake marketing activities.

Returning to synergy rule number three, we will remember that some targets are more effective than others. It is a basic premise that those with which we have personal relationships—such as present customers—are more likely to purchase from us again and again. This is exactly why large institutions purchase other institutions. Banks purchase other banks to increase their present customer base. They can build "bricks and mortar" much more cheaply than by purchasing branches—but these new branches do not come with an instant customer base.

Having a customer base and fully utilizing such to its full potential is another matter. Anyone who lives in a home knows that it is not unusual to receive two or three solicitations for credit cards in the mail each day. Each one has an offer that seems to top the last offer: *8.9% fixed or a free trip on the Star Trek*

Enterprise. But are these offers valuable to those being wooed? Are they enough to keep the recipients from calling their present bank when they would like to add another credit instrument?

It is only through the offering of value that we really get people to act incongruent to the way they are typically disposed to act. A direct mail campaign to a zip code or to a targeted demographic profile is a cold call activity—no matter how targeted. At this point we must choose between a smaller response rate of those who are interested in purchasing (act on this offer now) and a larger response rate of those who are interested in the general area of service we can provide (call for a special report). Those generally interested may not be ready to purchase anything at this juncture. If we choose the lower response rate, the next time we mail we will again be mailing cold to a group that has not received value from our institution. The larger response rate gives us the ability to build up a database of potential clients with whom we are beginning to develop a relationship. This is not quite as strong as previous customers, but we have invoked the *law of reciprocity* with these respondents because we have given them something of value without expecting anything in return.

Of course, the *law of reciprocity* puts us in the position to garner something in return—future business or referrals to others who might be in a position to use our products or services. In order to take advantage of this position, we must consider a method of contact that will allow the one-to-one interaction necessary to achieve value in return. Offering value through automated systems such as fax on demand services limits our personal contact with potential clients. These systems may not put us in a position to garner referrals and may prevent us from doing just that.

The identification of our value instrument represents a major business decision. Many never add value to their marketing efforts because they do not identify where their value lies—or more importantly where they are unique as compared to the competition. Our uniqueness as a marketing tool is a concept we will investigate in more detail within chapter five.

Creating synergy is the key to an effective plan of action. The reason that we plan is to create a more effective approach. This can only happen if each of our efforts are linked in such a way that we can take advantage of all opportunities created.

CHAPTER TWO
The Traits You Must Have In Order To Achieve Maximum Synergy

*"Things may come to those who wait,
but only things left by those who hustle."*
Abraham Lincoln

All the planning in the world will not help if you do not execute. In fact, there are those who are prone to spend too much time planning and this prevents the time necessary for execution. Those who spend too much time planning are said to have a form of *call reluctance* in the field of sales analysis.

In a world of *planners* and *doers*, there is no doubt the planet belongs to the *doers*. After all, it is the *doers* who accomplish the task. We hope that those who follow the guidance set forth in this book with regard to developing marketing plans will not be encouraged to stay home and plan to a fault. Those who stay at home and think the majority of the time will not reap any rewards. Those who do will reap rewards. Our hope with this publication is that those who take action will stop and plan to make their actions more effective.

For every person exhibiting massive call reluctance there is another acting blindly in such a way that their actions bring little reward. These people are on the proverbial *treadmills* of life. For every two steps forward, they take one step backward. It is time these people turn the treadmill in reverse—getting two steps of results for every positive step taken. We do not at all expect less action, just more results. This is what synergy is all about.

Before we begin by identifying the planning steps, marketing tools and sales skills necessary to implement the maximum synergy rules, our first course of action is to identify ourselves as either *over-planners* or *blind doers*. Before we dive into building a plan and identifying out actions, we first must know what kind of person must implement that plan in order for the plan to be effective. By being cognizant of the traits of top performers, we can assess the areas we need for personal improvement and managers can assess the needs of their organizations. It is not enough to set up a plan to improve. Unless we have matched the right characteristics of a person and an organization together with that plan, there is very little hope for increased effectiveness within the implementation stage.

There are many positive traits exhibited by top producers. In this chapter, we will present some of the basic building blocks of performance. As in all other aspects of synergy, these traits are linked in such a way that you cannot exhibit one positive trait without possessing other positive traits. For example, a positive attitude leads to other attributes such as hard work. There is nothing like a negative attitude to inhibit the effort level of a person or an organization.

A positive attitude, honesty, hard work, professionalism and more. These are the building blocks upon which success is built for all companies and individuals within those companies. If you cannot honestly say that you are described as the epitome of these traits, your first goals are set. No synergistic marketing, management or customer service actions will help if the foundation is not in existence from which to build. These traits are limiting factors. If you do not excel in these areas, your actions will not work—no matter how they are linked.

This book is not a motivational work. Motivational works exist to help you achieve personal states you cannot achieve on your own (or help you help yourself achieve these states). It is our belief that motivational books, tapes and/or seminars are only temporary fixes.

Our goal is to help you recognize the traits. It will be your task to recognize where you need improvement and how you will effect that improvement. Acquiring the traits is another matter, and only you can help yourself acquire these traits.

A positive attitude

The importance of a positive attitude.

No trait is more important than the right attitude. A positive attitude sees a problem as a challenge. A positive attitude takes a loss and strives for improvement from that juncture. A positive attitude focuses on the *can dos*. A negative person is hampered by all obstacles. There are a million reasons one can become successful. There are also a million reasons that one can fail. The key is to focus on your advantages.

The existence of a positive attitude can lift an entire organization—especially if this attitude starts from the top and permeates downward. Conversely, a negative attitude from one or more individuals can hamper the effectiveness of a whole operation.

For example, a salesperson may focus on the organization's price disadvantages. With a focus on price, the salesperson cannot be effective. Of course, the salesperson is not succeeding and is obligated to let everyone know they are failing because the company is deficient—even as there are others succeeding in the same company with the same price. The operational people hear this constantly and are unable to differentiate fact from fiction because they are not part of the sales process. They believe the company is selling at a disadvantage. When the inside support staff is confronted with customer service challenges, they truly believe that someone else may be better. Why should our customers feel that our company is better if we do not sound that way in our responses, either in person or over the phone? The cycle begins to drag us down.

By the same token, a positive sales force keeps focusing on its market advantages such as features, services and benefits and has the operational staff believing the same. The inside force becomes more effective in selling the company and perpetuating sales as an ally of the sales personnel. When the whole organization is selling for the company the entire organization becomes stronger.

Recognizing a negative attitude

No one would argue with the premise that a positive attitude enhances the performance of everyone. The problem is that no one seems to recognize that they have a negative attitude. How can it be that there are so many negative attitudes surrounding us and no one will take responsibility for the negative atmosphere? Some believe that the negative attitudes are caused by external forces.

"I would be able to sell the company if the market was better"

These people do not recognize that a negative attitude is not acceptable under any circumstances. They are focusing upon things that they cannot control. Stephen R. Covey, in *The 7 Habits of Highly Effective People* (Simon & Schuster, 1989), would say that that person is influenced by his/her *circle of concern*, rather than the *circle of control*. When someone focuses on their *circle of control* by being proactive, it becomes larger as compared with their *circle of concern*. Since an attitude is always controllable from within, top performers focus within their own sphere of influence. You cannot control the markets or the competition. However, you can control your attitude concerning the markets and how you adjust your marketing plan to deal with changes in market conditions.

Still others do not believe that their attitude is negative or is in any way a concern regarding their productivity or the productivity of those surrounding them. They recognize that a negative attitude is counter-productive. They just do not see that particular attitude emanating from within.

Do you need an attitudinal checkup?

You can't understand it. You have had all the right training. You would like to make a lot of money. The market is strong and it supports people who transact more business than you. These people don't seem to be as talented as you. Every month you say that you will break through. Yet, it does not happen. What is wrong?

Is time for an attitudinal check-up? If there are those in your market who are outperforming you, the answer is YES! Here are some of the questions you should ask:

Do you want to make a lot of money but don't really want to help people? Most salespeople want to make more money. For this reason, when we hire we try to measure *money motivation.* The top salespeople are motivated to make even more money—but they are also motivated to help people.

It doesn't matter if you are selling real estate, legal services or any other product. You cannot sell to inanimate objects. You must sell to people. If you are not interested in learning these people's needs, developing relationships or otherwise helping these people obtain their goals, then you are doomed to failure before you start.

Whether your customer is a corporation or an individual, if you see yourself as their partner you are on the right track. If you see them as an impediment to your goals, you are going to languish in the basement of opportunity. Don't want to sell to people? Then try getting on the Internet and taking orders on a computer!

Are you held back by call reluctance? Everyone has call reluctance—if you don't have some feeling holding you back before you make a call, you wouldn't be normal. Some have studied the topic of call reluctance as a science. Dudley and Goodson in *Earning What You're Worth? The Psychology of Sales Call Reluctance* (Dudley, Goodson and Barnett Behavior Sciences Research Press, 1995 edition) identify the 12 faces of call reluctance. We will attempt to keep our discussion much simpler.

If you are producing less than you would like and are making less effective sales calls than you would like, you are undoubtedly hampered by call reluctance. Note, we emphasize the word *effective*. If you are constantly calling on a *safe target* (one you know well but cannot sell) and come away with nothing, you are not really making sales calls.

The only excuse for not making enough effective sales calls is that you are overloaded with business and you are trying to service that business. Even in these cases, those with a minimum of call reluctance will actually hire assistants to make sure their present business does not interfere with their marketing.

Do you really want to succeed? How do you overcome call reluctance? If you really want to succeed, then you will do what is necessary to force yourself to make the calls. As a matter of fact, those who are making calls are not forcing themselves, they are doing what comes naturally in the process of succeeding. If you let your call reluctance take over, than your urge to succeed just isn't strong enough.

Is there a potion to take to overcome lack of desire? Absolutely not—but the moment you accept this explanation and stop blaming other things such as training or the market, you can start building a solution. This solution may take a re-evaluation of all your priorities. Only you can really reach within yourself and come up with a priority list of what is important. If you feel that success in your line of work really is at the top of the list, then you must adjust your actions to make it happen. This means making effective sales calls.

Do you really want to succeed now? If you really want to succeed, do you really want to succeed today? Those who want to do it today are said to have a *sense of urgency*. If you really want to succeed, what is going to make tomorrow any different? Procrastination is what got you here in the first place. The only right time to take action is NOW!

Start breaking the cycle

Attitude will figure in every equation of performance, so if you are honest with yourself it may be time for a change. Faced with three alternatives for action: *Stay with the status quo, get on the right track,* or *find another vocation—* which do you choose?

There is only one wrong choice: *Stay with the status quo*

Under-performance is one thing. Acceptance of mediocrity is a whole new ball game. Nothing can cause your attitude to get worse than failure to reach your goals. And the worse your attitude becomes, the more you will tend to underperform. It is a vicious cycle. No one ever went from failure to success by sticking with the status quo. The time to break this cycle is now—*if* you really want to succeed.

How to break the cycle. The first step in breaking a cycle of under-performance is being honest. If you really want to succeed, you will take the actions necessary to bring success. If you don't *really* want success, you will tend to stick with exactly what you are doing now. If you *really* want success, take an accounting of what you *really* need to do:

- Do you need to change a negative attitude to positive?
- Do you need to go from being hampered by call reluctance to surpassing all obstacles?
- Do you need to find out where the business really is and continuously attack on all fronts?

If you are not succeeding and you don't think that you need a change in these three areas, you are not being honest with yourself. It is now time to enlist the help of others. Choose some mentors such as your boss, peers (especially top producers), family and targets.

Ask them to be painfully honest. This is important because your inner circle will not want to hurt your feelings. Just because you are not a top producer does not mean that they don't like you. You must convince them that you want only feedback that will improve performance. You are not interested in affirmation of any positive aspects of your execution since any positive affirmation will only point you back to the status quo. You may even choose to abandon some positive aspects of your game plan to accomplish more in the long run.

If people are being honest, you will hear statements such as:

You seem to miss larger opportunities that are presented because of smaller obstacles.

You focus on the negative aspects of your job.

You don't seem to be able to solve complex problems.

You seem to hang around the office too much.

Using the information. The purpose of this research is not to make you feel bad and cause your attitude to get worse. The reason that we ask an alcoholic to announce their disease is to begin the road to recovery.

The solutions for your recovery are quite simple. If you need to go where the business *really* is, then find out where it is. If you don't know, ask your boss or top producing peers. Every office or company has top producing individuals from whom the information is readily available. You do not have to reinvent the wheel. The process of *benchmarking* uses the knowledge of those around us. Take a top producer out to lunch. Spend a day with them. Volunteer to be their assistant for one month. If you don't know the answers, become a sponge for good information instead of a mediocre complainer stuck in the muck of the status quo.

What if you really don't want success? If you really don't want success, then the time for honesty is now. Salaried workers in the government sector may be able to reach retirement by coasting. Not so for commissioned sales personnel. There is nothing wrong with recognizing that you are in the wrong industry—or wrong aspect of the industry. It is wrong to not recognize that fact and continuously be miserable because you are underperforming with regard to your expectations.

If you can be happy in a salaried job with delineated responsibilities—then take action to achieve that position. *The key is happiness.* If your happiness comes through accomplishing independent successes in a self-directed career, then take the actions necessary to achieve your goals. There is no greater reward than that.

Five ways to improve your attitude

Recognize that it is not everyone else. The first step is to recognize yourself for what you are. Alcoholics Anonymous is the number one training program in the United States (unfortunately), and the first step of the program is to admit that you are an alcoholic. The first step to a better attitude is to admit it is not everyone else's attitude that stinks—it is yours that needs adjusting. Really serious about improving your attitude? Spend some time asking people to be brutally honest about what they think of yours. Without this step, the other ways are virtually worthless.

Recognize that you are responsible. While bad attitudes are contagious, only you can give yourself a better attitude. All the motivational tapes and pep talks in the world will actually have a negative effect if you feel that there is an external fix (our apologies to those big, motivational superstar trainers). If you find yourself saying that you would be happier if this or that happened— forget it. The only thing that must happen is that you recognize you are responsible for your own state of mind.

Stay away. Do you know someone else who literally lights up a room when they leave it? Stay away from those people, they are negativities and they can only lead you further from your goal. Somehow it seems comforting to share woes with other people—after all, misery loves company. In the long run, you will be the misery keeping everyone else company.

Be healthy. It is hard to feel good about life when you feel miserable inside. How many of you feel chipper when nursing a huge hangover? Probably none. Stop smoking. Lose weight. Exercise. Drink moderately, if at all. You have heard it all before. When you resolve to take these things seriously, you will actually lift your attitude in two ways. When you accomplish something such as a good workout, you will feel better about yourself. And when you generally feel good, a better attitude will soon follow.

Improve your mind. It is said that increasing your *aptitude* will elevate your *attitude* that will raise your *altitude.* Nothing will cause your attitude to wallow in the mud more than a stagnant mind. Learn something and you will have cause to feel that you are moving through life on an incline rather than moving through life on a treadmill.

We could easily list more ways to improve your attitude. For example, what about spending more time doing fun things and just enjoying life? How about time dedicated to determining your main direction in life (where are you going and how to get there). Just conquering these first five will put you in a position to really make a difference in your life. Try it—what do you have to lose but that old sour outlook on life?

Asking—do you do it consistently?

The world is full of people and companies who seem to do everything right but never achieve success:

> *"He has all the talent in the world and works hard.*
> *I don't understand why he is not leading the pack."*

Top producers have a hard time relating to people who work hard but do not want the business badly enough to ask for it. Why would anyone stay in a job and not want the business? Hard to believe, but it is true. How does one make sure that they do not get enough business to be a top performer and only enough to keep them in their position? They don't ask!

There are only two reasons that a person does not ask for the business:

1) They are not putting themselves in position to ask for the business. They do not put themselves in position because they either are not working hard enough to get in position or they do not know how to put themselves in position. One could argue that the state of being uninformed is really one of lack of desire. If one did not know how to get the business, one would find out the keys to successful positioning if they really wanted success badly enough. This is why some are successful with almost no background or training (going back to attitude). Do you ever wonder why some salespeople make calls constantly on low producing customers who do not have business to refer? This is a *comfort call.*

2) They are in position, but are not asking because they do not really desire the business. These people are called *perpetual callers.* Some never learn how to call because of a lack of desire to succeed. Others go through the motions of calling but never follow through enough to procure the business.

Regardless of the reason why the person is not asking, it is a basic tenant of business that you will not achieve success without asking for results. Business does not float in the door unless you have the lowest prices in your field. Those who have the lowest prices may need to get the word out, but do not need to sell. The world of top performers is not populated by order-takers, it is populated by those who procure additional business for themselves and their employers.

Can you get over rejection and move on?

Rejection is an important part of the sales process. It is not true that the best salespeople do not get rejected. They may get rejected more because they ask more. Many who have call reluctance do not want to experience rejection. You can ease the sting of rejection by achieving other goals such as referrals to other prospects. This is more likely if you are networking rather than cold calling. The best way to overcome the sting of rejection is to succeed. This means listening and doing a needs assessment so that you ask at the right time—when you can add value. It also means that you pick yourself up after a rejection and call again. Nothing helps more than tasting success as well as rejection. Great salespeople learn from each success and each rejection so that their next call is more effective. That is why another trait of success is flexibility, which leads us to the next section on change.

Change—are you ready for the 21st Century?

In his book, *GOD Wants You To Be Rich*, noted economist and author Paul Zane Pilzer (March, 1997) studies the history of the speed of change. Some of his statements could be very scary to those who don't read further:

> *The speed of change: Fifty years ago it took a*
> *lifetime for technology to make your job irrelevant.*
> *Now, it's just five years.*

While it did take 50 years for the U.S. to go from having 30 million farmers to fewer than three million, it now takes just a few years for certain technologies (such as the carburetor) to change in such a way that significant career shifts are commonplace. Should we run into our homes and hide until we find out how all of this will play out? Not unless we have a computer inside!

The point is: with every change comes a significant opportunity. The losers in this world will be those who are resistant to change itself. The winners will be those who are easily adaptable to new technologies and associated trends.

This may not necessarily mean career changes every five years for those who would like to get ahead. However, it may mean major changes in the way they perform their job—especially for those who deal with the public.

It is time to ask the question . . .

Are you resistant to change? Do you feel that you are always in transition and you can't stand the thought of another year of chaos? Or, do you actively look for ways to change your life—to improve the way you accomplish every day tasks?

Measuring your change quotient is more complex than determining how long you have worked for a particular company in one position. It means examining everything you do and how you react to certain environmental stimuli.

When a new computer program is introduced in your office, do you:

- ◆ Become the first to get hooked up and see how it can help you function?
- ◆ Cautiously watch others spend their time experimenting and jump in when the system is free of bugs?

- ◆ Hire someone to integrate the program into your system and teach you how to push the right button?
- ◆ Hide under your desk and pray that the program does not leave the computer and start eating the three thousand sticky notes on your desk?

Which is the right answer? It may not be the most effective move to jump on the computer and then spend three days experimenting and hoping to discover the right formula. Those who are successful are not necessarily going to be those who invent the new technologies. It is going to be those who determine how to better utilize these technologies in such a way that our jobs and lives will be easier.

Did Gates invent the point and click programming that brought Windows to millions of households? Or, did he see a great technology on another system and determine that the opportunity was there for the asking? The rest is history!

Your task is not to reinvent the wheel. Your task is to recognize that the wheel is being reinvented again and again in today's fast paced environment. This means that you must determine how the new wheel can make you go faster, be more efficient, reach more customers or be a force in new markets.

And you must make these determinations quickly because newer technologies will close windows of opportunities with great alacrity. If you don't put your foot through the door, someone else will. There is no field that will not be greatly affected by this phenomenon. If you stay in a stagnant position, you will fall behind faster and faster.

On the other hand, if you decide to be a leader in today's changing world, the opportunities will be endless. Remember when you thought, I can't believe that I missed that great investment opportunity? Now you can witness a new revolution every few years and with each revolution will come countless new opportunities. We have never had a period that held so much promise out to enterprising individuals. We also have never had another period that was bringing change to the forefront on so many levels.

One trait you will have to master in this ever-changing world is flexibility. The faster the rate of change, the more flexible you will have to be. In the past one may have been able to succeed keeping the status quo in place— but in the future this stance will become harder and harder. You cannot successfully implement any of our maximum synergy rules without the flexibility necessary to adapt within the present and future era of change.

Communication

Communication is the key to implementing all of our synergy rules. Therefore, we discuss communication extensively throughout this work. Here are some examples of areas in which we must communicate.

- ◆ the organization's goals;
- ◆ an employee's responsibilities;
- ◆ how we can help a customer obtain their objectives;
- ◆ what we would like a prospect to do in certain situation;
- ◆ progress towards our goals;
- ◆ company policies;
- ◆ industry and product trends;
- ◆ how to obtain certain information; and,
- ◆ competitive positioning.

Our marketing represents, in effect, ways to communicate with our target audience. Later in this book we will spend some time establishing that public speaking is an excellent synergy tool. Public speaking is an advanced form of communication. Networking represents a controlled facilitation of communication with regard to our present sphere of influence. Cold calling represents a controlled facilitation of communication with regard to prospects outside of our present sphere of influence.

Not everyone possesses great communication skills. Some lack verbal skills and others lack written skills. Still others do not communicate well with their body language. It is important to note that our goals should include the improvement of these skills where necessary. You can have the best intentions in the world, but if you cannot communicate these intentions clearly, your efforts will go to waste.

Many conflicts we witness are due to poor communication occurring somewhere in the sales or management processes. For example, if I am a lawyer and I promise that I can win a case and then the case is not won—I effectively have promised more than I can deliver. If a manager indicates that a salesperson can earn $100,000 their first year and the average for the first year is actually $40,000, what is the chance that the employee will be disappointed?

Another common example of poor communication skills occurs when a sales or operations person does not let a customer know when a problem occurs during the delivery process. This might occur during the processing of a loan application or trying to effect a furniture delivery. All too often we feel that we can solve the problem so we don't let the customer know until the last minute and all hope is lost. The worst time to let a customer know there may be a problem is at the last minute before delivery is supposed to take place. Imagine learning that you are not moving into your new home the day before the move is to take place!

There is no doubt that great communication skills can help us succeed in today's fast paced world. Those who hold great sales meeting or seminars possess a significant advantage over those who cannot communicate to groups effectively. Those who can deliver their message effectively on paper are more likely to effect action from their target audiences. Those who communicate honestly and consistently with their customers are more likely to receive repeat business and additional referrals. This is why communication skills should be an integral part of all management and sales training programs.

Flexibility

We have already established that change will bring great challenges and opportunities for those in business. If we take a look back in time, we can gain a perspective as to just how important flexibility will be in our future. As we progress from year to year, there is no way that we can see what is happening around us in the long term. In order to gain a more accurate perspective, we must take a step back and look at the bigger picture. For example, look at the year 1899. What do you see?

We had just invented the light bulb and telephone. Most people were not even touched by these inventions by the turn of the Century. The automobile was a novel dream and the airplane was more far-fetched than that!

Almost two decades later we were fighting a war, which featured the destructive side of all of these inventions. By the middle of the century, our destructive capabilities had reached proportions not even dreamed of 50 years before.

The automobile and electricity transformed America from a rural country to one with bustling cities and suburbs. In the 1920s, a large drought contributed to a worldwide depression. Today, agriculture still feeds our population, but agricultural companies do not dominate business headlines.

If change has caused the face of the world to change in the past 100 years, what will it do during the next 100 years? Technology is advancing at such a rapid speed, if you blink you will be existing in the past. Today's personal computers contain more power and speed than the mainframes powering whole governments 25 years ago, when the computer was invented.

In the future, we will be able to bring information to each citizen that could not have been in the dreams of our grandparents. Medical advances are following and major diseases such as cancer and diabetes are sure to be conquered in the next century, just as polio and small pox were conquered within industrial countries in the past century.

From agriculture to industry to technology, we must be prepared for change in the coming years. The consumers we service will go through adjustments in months that previously took years to develop and study. They will be looking for speed, convenience and instant gratification.

For a demonstration of this capacity for change, take a good look at the economic events of the past ten years. We have had the longest economic boom in the history of America. Interest rates and unemployment were the lowest in decades. Yet, month by month, the markets became spooked by the specter of inflation, rates spike continually and the stock market demonstrated extreme volatility with spectacular rises and just as significant corrections.

With regular stock market corrections rivaling the size of the 1929 crash that triggered the largest depression in history, where do we go from here? Well, consumers adjust and start purchasing using tools available today that they would never have turned to in the past—such as adjustable rate mortgages. After all, they can always refinance 12 months from now. They also purchase stocks that will perform better during periods of slower growth or place their money in banks or indexed mutual funds. In other words, the consumer adjusts and moves on.

What this means to a business person is that if you don't make quick adjustments in the future, your customers will leave you just as quickly. The acquisition of business is very expensive. In the future, it will take an extreme amount of flexibility in the form of changing business strategies in order to keep your customers in the fold for the long term.

Goal orientation

You are not likely to reach the pinnacle of success unless you truly have defined what success means to you. If success is defined in terms of the achievement of goals set out by others, you will be striving for a plateau that has been built for someone else. This is not to say that reaching the plateau will not bring a great sense of accomplishment. However, how many times have you heard of people achieving milestones and still not feeling content? This may be because they have not spent enough time defining their own goals in life. The goals may have delineated through interaction with their parents, spouses, bosses and/or peers—rather than their own ideals and needs.

When your actions are truly coordinated toward the achievement of goals that are meaningful within your own sense of achievement, these actions are likely to have more impact. These goals must be delineated for all facets of your life, including:

◆ long-term goals (such as retirement) vs. short-term goals (such as what you would like to accomplish tomorrow); and,

◆ monetary goals (how much would you like to make next year) versus non-monetary goals (such as recognition).

Arriving at these definitions will help you not be one of those who are seemingly doing well but are "missing something" in their life. They have not defined what they want to accomplish in their jobs and what affect this accomplishment may have on their personal lives. Organizations are no less needful of the same goal orientation. Many companies drift from quarter to quarter looking for a maximum profit and ignoring long-term industry trends that may be eroding their competitive positions.

We will be spending more time upon the topic of goals when we start delineating the components of a marketing plan within the next chapter. In order to successfully build the components of a plan, one must start by having a goal orientation. That is, their actions must be guided by the achievement of certain objectives set out from within.

Hard work

Schemes to get rich quick by mailing a few letters are prevalent in the back of many periodicals. If they really worked, there would be many more rich people in the world—including those who run the advertisements. The fact of the matter is that most fortunes are accumulated through hard work over long periods of time. In the new eras of technology and competition, this statement is truer than ever. We must constantly work to keep ahead of our competition.

"It takes 20 years to become an overnight success."

Eddie Cantor

Not everyone is willing to pay the price of success. If you are not willing or able, it is important to be honest with yourself and those around you. There is plenty of room for those who subsist within the masses. If you are not honest concerning your level of effort, you will be setting up a conflict within yourself. This conflict will rage constantly as you wonder why you are not successful. External forces such as your pricing and the market will be substituted as logical alternatives.

The truth of the matter is that those who join the elite are few and far between:

"Excellent things are rare."
Plato

People emerge from the masses through a positive attitude and hard work. If one feels that they should be part of the elite and are held back by others, they will never be satisfied. You can feel like a success if you attain the level of production that you feel your level of effort has brought to bear. On the other hand, you will always believe you are a failure if you feel that you are working hard and achieving less.

Hard work gives us an advantage over our competition in many ways:

It makes our efforts persistent. Though the numbers have been debated for ages, it is generally known that long-term sales are made after five to ten quality calls. We emphasize the word *quality* here because many make what we call *comfort calls* without any hope of success. A quality call is a call on someone who has business to acquire and with whom we take the steps necessary to procure that business. Most callers give up after two or three efforts. It is those who are willing to be persistent who will achieve their objectives. Those who are not persistent go to work on the next target after two or three calls and eventually give up calling because they are not reaping rewards for their efforts.

It makes our efforts consistent. Those who work hard can move in more than one direction without sacrificing their previous efforts. Those who are working only a few hours a day must abandon their previous efforts in order to take on a new venture.

Here is an example:

A direct mail campaign is begun to increase product sales. We then follow-up with three phone calls each day to set up appointments the following week. As the appointments take place, the phone calls may suffer—unless you are a peak performer who is willing to make the calls and have several meetings each day. Those who reach capacity quickly will suffer the *roller coaster effect* of production—production will tend to increase while visits are taking place. Then production will start to drop because phone calls were not made while visits were taking place. Phone calls begin again . . .

It draws top customers to you. If you desire to achieve a high level of success, you will want to be successful with the targets (companies or individuals) that tend to be the most successful in their field. Your top customers will therefore be those who are the hardest workers in your field. They prefer to do business with those whose work habits mirror themselves. Nothing is more of a turn-off to a top producer than personally witnessing a half-hearted sales effort.

Honesty

The practice of being *above board* means more than telling the truth or staying out of jail. It includes:

- ◆ not promising more than is likely to be delivered;
- ◆ not proffering advice within areas for which you are not qualified;
- ◆ not withholding information concerning the features of your product or services that may influence someone's decision;
- ◆ maintaining a reputation for business ethics that is a cut above the rest of the industry; and,
- ◆ admitting your own shortcomings to yourself so that you will work to improve what is necessary to achieve top performance.

You have to start being honest with yourself. Though only ten percent of the business world is made up of top producers, the other 90 percent believe that they have all the traits necessary to succeed. Of course, there are always external factors preventing their success:

"The market is lousy."
"Our product line is deficient."
"I have a terrible territory."
"I am just holding back."

Because they do not admit their shortcomings to themselves, they are never working to improve their deficiencies and have no hope to become top producers. This is why one must first be honest with oneself. This is a necessary step before the process of self-improvement can begin. Any of the traits of top producers can be achieved with a concerted effort for improvement.

Being honest with your customer base and staff is no less important. It is too easy to use falsehoods to make a deal happen:

"Of course, we can deliver in less than 30 days."

We may know full well that the 30-day delivery date has a probability of less than 50 percent. We may also know that someone else will step forward and make the claim if you do not. When we miss 50 percent of the time, the customer has a bad taste at the end of the transaction because you over-promised and under-delivered. Someone will now be in a position to pick up business because the relationship is not on solid ground. What is a proper response?

*"Anyone who definitely promises you a 30-day delivery
is not being totally honest. There are too many intervening
variables which can effect the final outcome. I will promise to
do as good a job as anyone in the industry in following up on
the delivery system in an effort to make sure your needs are met."*

Promising something we are not likely to deliver almost ensures that we will not exceed our customer's expectations. Promises are made by sales personnel frequently. These may be simple promises such as a phone call at a certain time. But each time a promise is not delivered upon, your clients or cohorts are not only inconvenienced, they are robbed of their most precious resource— time. You have forced them to make their decisions based upon false assumptions. In effect, you are taking money out of their pockets. In the law, the term for this activity is *criminal negligence.*

Offering advice beyond one's purview can be just as damaging. As a professional you may occupy a *fiduciary* relationship with your customer. A mortgage banker, Realtor®, personal banker or financial planner may be called upon to offer advice on the future direction of interest rates. The truth is that trained economists cannot predict the future of interest rates. Because the customer may value your opinion as a professional, they may ask you to delve beyond your realm of expertise. If they make significant financial decisions based upon your advice without you making a disclaimer as to the limitations, conflicts and disappointments are sure to be inevitable.

There is a second disadvantage to passing ourselves off as experts in many areas. We start relying upon ourselves rather than the real experts and as such we weaken our relationships with these experts. Our sphere of influence should be full of professionals trained in the areas in which we are not. Each of these professionals should represent opportunities for reciprocal referral relationships—basic synergy marketing.

So honesty is more than staying out of jail. Honesty is not trying to be something that we are not. We must stick to our area of expertise, because once the cycle is started it becomes difficult to break out. If one is really looking for a long-term, successful career, there is no real choice—take the high road!

Improvement

Salespeople tend to get lost fighting the fires of survival each day. We constantly win battles—making sale after sale—while we fall behind in the long-term war of success. One day we look up and we are hopelessly behind competitors who have launched new strategies that cause us to initiate a fire drill as we play catch up.

We tend to completely reengineer our overall plans once every five years, causing a major disruption in our lives, rather than trying to achieve a more sensible approach of continual improvement. When it comes to self-improvement, there are two significant guidelines to which we must adhere:

- ◆ We must improve constantly or we will be overwhelmed by our competition; and,
- ◆ Improvement must come gradually.

Try as we might, there is little chance to transform ourselves overnight. The state of gradual improvement is described by a Japanese word—*Kaizen.*

Let us assume that no one can afford to take a year off to revamp their business strategies and that we all must embark on continuous training in order to keep up in a rapidly evolving environment. Where do we start?

The opportunities for personal and professional improvement surround us and we must make ourselves sensitive to these opportunities. Here are some suggestions:

Develop objectives. In what areas do you feel that you need improvement? Talk to a few of your successful peers. In what areas do they possess expertise that you do not? Perhaps you would like to improve your public speaking capacity or you would like to increase your technical capabilities. Make a laundry list of topics and develop your priorities. Remember, you cannot take on all projects at one time.

Read Books. Take a ride to your local book store and in addition to picking up the latest mystery novel, peruse the personal improvement and business sections. Pick up a few books relevant to your topics. These books will be a great source of information and will also help us determine what long-term plan of action might take shape.

Peruse industry publications. The primary purpose of these organizations is the advancement of its membership. There are a variety of training and marketing materials and events made available to members—books, audio tapes, video tapes and seminars. Get involved in these organizations as they represent absolutely wonderful opportunities to network and learn about opportunities for improvement.

Start attending seminars. All to often, industry seminars are attended by those who are not transacting business while those who are doing business are too busy to attend. The truth is that each person needs a balance between business and learning experiences. If you are spending all of your time learning you are not accomplishing anything. You must achieve this delicate balance.

Spend time developing implementation strategies. Why don't we spend time improving? Because we cannot find the time. Fires use up our available time because they scream louder. To improve we must make it a priority to do so. Here are some examples of implementation strategies:

- ◆ *Use down time.* Most every salesperson spends a certain amount of time in the car. Purchase audio tapes and listen to them again and again. Instead of being up-tight because you can't get to your appointment by blowing through traffic, make your trip more enjoyable and productive.
- ◆ *Schedule your learning time.* Vow to spend a certain amount of time each week on learning activities. Schedule this time in your calendar. We already schedule meetings, doctors appointments, vacations and more, isn't learning time just as important? The time expended does not have to be substantial—try an hour each week. Real improvement comes a little at a time through consistent and persistent energy.
- ◆ *Make your next vacation an improvement experience.* Every time you go out of town to unwind, use the opportunity to take on an

improvement project. Take a book on honing marketing skills as well as a mystery novel. You will find the experience will renew your vigor as well as the snooze time at the beach.

After we find the methods necessary to achieve the improvement we are seeking, we will find that we can implement these methods through a variety of ways within our business lives—

Lift our attitude. We have already established that a great attitude is the key to success. It certainly is the key characteristic of any successful salesperson. Don't have a great attitude? How many people really do with the stress of today's existence? Ask yourself these questions:

Do others come to you to seek a lift?
Do you wish that life's many obstacles were out of your way?
Do you rely on motivational tapes to lift your spirits?

Most people think their attitude is great—or at least good. But if people are not coming to you for a lift and you are focused upon your own obstacles and others to provide a lift—there is much room for improvement. Think about how much more you could accomplish by making your attitude just ten percent better. And it's free.

Work a little harder. We don't expect that someone working 20 hours each week will read this section and become a 60-hour per week demon. Perhaps you could work ten percent harder and eliminate activities that are not helping you achieve your goals. Think about how much more this improvement could help you achieve in a lifetime.

Are you already stressed out from too much work? Don't assume that your ten percent premium must be applied to your workday. If your long-term goal is to make a difference in life, perhaps the time could be spent volunteering.

Develop a skill. There is no better way to get ahead than by developing a special skill that will give you the edge over the competition. Want to sell more? Become a public speaker. Or perhaps you could become an expert within an industry niche such as the tax advantages of particular investment vehicles.

If you try to sell all things to all people you will be competing with the world. Stop doing what the world is doing and develop your own style. When you do this you will become a leader instead of following the competition. Resolve to "go where none have gone before."

Decide upon a specific target. Speaking of selling all things to all people, narrow your efforts. Be known as an expert within a certain target group and become more specific within your marketing efforts. It takes much more energy and monetary resources to cast a net over a whole world versus going right to the source that can help you achieve your goals. Yes, less can help you achieve more.

Acquire the desire. We all say that we want to succeed, but few of us are willing to pay the price. How do you demonstrate that you are willing to make the sacrifices necessary to move ahead of the pack?

◆ *We ask everyone for the business.* We stop making excuses such as "this person is not interested" or "I can't ask my best friend or my spouse's boss." We ask everyone because if we play the game alone, we can't win the game.

◆ *We tell everyone what we want to accomplish.* When we stop being secretive and make public pronouncements, we start alliances that will help us become more successful. You will be surprised when you find out who will help.

◆ *We finally admit that we have met the enemy and it is ourselves* (Pogo). When we stop blaming all the obstacles we cannot control and focus on the one thing we can change, we gain the ability to make tremendous strides.

Look within and find the key to successful improvement. The changes we need to make may not be radical—but small adjustments can make a world of difference over a lifetime.

Knowledge

A successful business person is one who is knowledgeable in many areas:

Their company. A successful business person knows the history, direction, organization and all other aspects of their own company. How can you sell a company without knowing its strong and weak points? If they have failed in the past, why? How has this company learned and become stronger from failure? What levels of expertise are backing you or your department?

Their product. A successful business person must know their product or service from top to bottom. In this manner, the customer must look at you as the expert. If the product is only a portion of a larger discipline (for example, one particular investment in a field of investments), then knowledge of the larger picture is a necessity.

Their customer. Not only must a successful business person know how their product or service works, they must also be an expert on how that product will benefit their target. In order to do this, you must learn as much as possible about how your customer operates. Becoming an expert in their field will give you better ideas about how you can add value to your customers and it will enable you to communicate on their level. Nothing turns a customer off faster than speaking industry related language and having to translate to an outsider. You should become part of their inner circle.

Sales techniques. A successful business person is a student of sales and is constantly learning marketing and closing techniques. This is most important in the exploding area of automation. If one is not learning how automation will be affecting their market and marketing efforts, they are likely to be left behind in the near future.

The competition. A successful business person does not ignore the competition. Instead of complaining about price or relationship disadvantages, they learn all the strong and weak points of their competition. This gives them an advantage when going head-to-head, especially since their competition is not likely to do the same amount of research.

It is advisable to develop a relationship with your competition. There is much to be said for the process of *benchmarking*—finding out what others are doing well and duplicating these efforts rather than reinventing the wheel. If this research uncovers a service or product you provide that your competition does not (and vice-versa), you may even want to set up a referral relationship. In this way you can benefit from your competition's contacts. Many are afraid to lose their customers through referring them to another service. Remember, your customers will obtain the service you are missing from someone else, but if you make the connection first, you are adding to the value you provide for your customer:

"If I can't do it, I have a relationship with someone who can."

Knowledge—adding value through sharing expertise

Want to be seen as more than a "pushy" salesperson? You are not alone. It is the goal of most salespeople to be seen as more than just someone peddling goods. We would like to be described as one who:

◆ delivers high quality service;
◆ fills needs of our clients; and,

◆ adds value to the lives of our clients.

The question remains: If we are selling for a living, how do we move from being thought of as a salesperson to being thought of as a consultant? Even more significantly, how do we move up to the role of *industry expert*?

To be thought of as an expert, we must change the perception of those to whom we sell. We have to elevate ourselves in their eyes. We have to bring value to their lives.

There is nothing that brings more value to people's lives then being a teacher or mentor. Bestow your wisdom to your clientele and the rewards will be great for you and for them. It does not matter what you are selling, for example:

◆ If you are selling homes, teach the tax benefits of owning or how to leverage your investment;

◆ If you are selling cars, teach ways to preserve the value of one's cars;

◆ If you are selling insurance, teach how to prevent losses in case of a natural disaster (and personal safety as well); or,

◆ If you are selling financial investments, teach your clients how to protect their assets.

The topic is not as important as the fact that it enriches the lives of those who learn and creates synergy with your designated product (this does not mean that the topic actually sells your product). The more value you bestow, the higher your perception in the eyes of your clients. Why would any of your clients deal with a salesperson when they could be dealing with an expert?

You say that you have always wanted to teach but you are just not comfortable with the topic? Or perhaps you are not comfortable speaking in public?

Regarding the first challenge, remember that the topic does not have to be complex. Those attending your seminars are not professionals in your field and if your delivery is too complex they will become confused. In addition, you do not have to teach the topic by yourself. For example, if you are in real estate and you are speaking on the topic of tax benefits, call upon a Certified Public Accountant and divide the curriculum so that you appear as experts together. When you do this you are in a position to setup a reciprocal referral relationship with the professional with whom you are sharing the stage. This is what synergy is all about.

Despite the fact that your topics and material need not be complex, they do need to be organized and they need to help others achieve their own goal of being more financially secure. What may seem mundane to you is fascinating to others who are not within your field of expertise.

Not comfortable speaking in public? You are not alone. Public speaking is one of the greatest fears in America. There is a great organization dedicated to helping those with this fear increase their speaking skills—Toastmasters. Most areas have a local chapter. We will discuss this topic in more detail within Chapter 5.

The best practice for training your clientele? Start as a mentor to someone within your industry. Remember who helped you out when you started? Nothing will boost your confidence more than knowing you are helping someone with his or her career. The topics you teach them will make an excellent basis for putting together training seminars.

As a matter of fact, it would not be out of the question to assign the task of putting together an outline of such a seminar to your student. Have them sit through a dry run of the topic and comment on the value as part of their training. In this way you can deliver value to more than one party at one time.

Yes, we are all trying to earn more money in sales. We rate our success based on how we do versus the competition (*The Number One Agent in* _____). Most of us would like to achieve more than financial success, we would like to know that we are providing value to the world. Sharing our expertise is an excellent way to do both.

Persistence

In order to achieve long-term success, one's sales efforts must be persistent. Earlier we discussed our marketing activities being consistent. Marketing activities can be consistent, but they cannot be persistent. Only a person can be persistent.

In other words, a newsletter can be sent to your targets consistently, but they cannot achieve persistence. A person can pursue their goals relentlessly. A person can be tenacious. A flyer or a newspaper cannot.

You may get the impression that we are advising salespeople to be pushy and aggressive—playing into the public stereotype of a salesperson who is a tacky, pushy individual. In truth, persistence does not relate to these characteristics in any shape or form.

Persistence relates to a mindset or attitude. It means that we will never give up. A great salesperson understands that they will not sell everyone (all objections cannot be answered). Yet, they do not let obstacles get in the way of achieving their objectives.

Persistence means returning calls promptly and following up on schedule. It does not mean calling 15 times each day and making a nuisance of yourself. Persistence means getting up each day and making calls whether yesterday was a bad day or not. Persistence means getting to the bottom of an objection and understanding your client's needs instead of arguing or just giving up.

If one wants to know about the importance of persistence, just take a look at these estimates from the Association of Professional Salesmen—

2% of sales are made on the 1st contact
3% of sales are made on the 2nd contact
5% of sales are made on the 3rd contact
10% of sales are made on the 4th contact
80% of sales are made on the 5th-12th contact

Persistence is an excellent trait. While some mistake persistence for aggressiveness, we may be splitting hairs by making a distinction. We relate aggressiveness to someone who is likely to attack rather than someone who is likely to stick to a plan and see it through the implementation and evaluation stages. Persistence is a trait that is essential for a successful salesperson.

Professionalism

You have heard it a thousand times. To succeed in today's changing environment, you must be a professional. Traditional methods of selling will not work in a climate of advanced technology that is causing continual reevaluations of the needs of today's consumers. Not only are the needs changing constantly, so are the players.

What is a professional salesperson and why will this prototype be absolutely necessary as we begin a new century? Everyone seems to define professionalism from a different point of view, but most would agree on the following essential ingredients:

The professional has a vision. Rather than wandering aimlessly through life trying to cope with one day at a time, the professional has a definitive vision of the future. It is this vision that guides the professional through his/her career.

The professional can envision a business world that is entirely different from the one a traditional business person sees before them today. Actions are intended as preparation for winning in a new environment that may be radically different from the world that exists today.

Those who attempt to conquer only the tasks directly ahead of them may not be in a position to view each step as moving them away from where they will need to be weeks, months and years from today. Instead of building upon their achievements, they start over each day on a treadmill—and continue to press on until their energy level wears down.

The professional has goals. A vision of the future does not serve much purpose unless this vision includes your standing in any new environment. You must know where you desire to be in the long run as well as where you would like to be today. This statement of goals must include your ultimate role—both professional and personal—and what you would like to achieve through those roles. The actions of today's professionals are intended to move one closer to the ultimate achievement of one's ultimate objectives in another dimension.

Much has been said of goals with regard to their role in guiding the mission of success. Goals can become ineffective when we set them and there is no ultimate reward of achievement. A professional prevents goals from becoming meaningless by delineating objectives that stretch their achievements but can be and are attained. It is the reward of achievement that motivates us towards setting and achieving long-term goals that are more meaningful to our careers. In other words, a true professional elevates the role of objectives by giving these objectives existence through their continual achievement each and every day. *Kaisen* means growing a little better each day.

The professional has ethics. A discussion of the importance of goals can sometimes lead us to believe that the achievement of these objectives is the ultimate objective—at any price. A professional cannot afford to be Machiavellian in the implementation phase because that professional will lose a most important attribute—respect. The professional must be able to compete on an even playing field with his/her competition and not cut corners. All sales-people occupy a position of trust in the minds of their customers and peers. If this trust is violated, the achievement of an objective may actually mean the loss of long-term aspirations.

In this regard, ethics denote more than following the letter of the law. It means conducting oneself in such a way that we are always *above board*. For example, many business people are tempted to promise more than can be delivered in order to overcome objections brought forward by their targets. When these promises evaporate, the salesperson hopes to have a long-term lock on the future relationship. Losing business to someone who is extending these promises presents a special problem to those who don't expect to cross the line. It appears that those lacking ethics are winning the war, but in truth, your targets will gravitate to those they can respect in the long run. You may very well lose a battle, but the ultimate goal will be achieved by those who are respected throughout their industry.

The professional has a plan. Achieving success in a rapidly changing and increasingly competitive marketplace takes more than the execution of a random set of actions. The professional seeks to increase their marketing effectiveness by coordinating their actions in such a way that the chance of success is maximized. A professional marketing plan includes a careful identification of targets, the selection of tools to reach these targets and the implementation of a set of actions designed to achieve maximum diversity and synergistic efficiency.

A diversified marketing plan is especially important in an evolving market. Too many have not been able to achieve long-term success because they were too busy surviving day-to-day as rapid changes put them continually behind. Diversity means strength because changes are met with actions that are easily adaptable to these changes. You are now ahead of the curve of change and are able to set your sights on the next level of achievement.

The significance of synergy is understood in terms of resources. Everyone has a limited amount of precious resources available to them. It is those who are more effective in the use of these resources who will achieve maximum success. Synergy ensures that all actions are coordinated in such a way that they will feed upon each other. The formula of one plus one now equals a result of three—because you are increasing your everyday effectiveness.

The professional's plan includes value for their targets. The most important component of a professional's plan is the action that adds value to their target. Much has been said concerning the concept of value-added with regard to marketing. It is easy to understand that a salesperson who adds more value than their competitors will possess a distinct advantage in the market place. However, the objective is difficult to achieve because it involves a specific determination of need from the target. It would be typical for a target not to be entirely focused on ways that a solicitor might add value to their business.

Developing a system for added value will involve significant study and preparation for any individual. Benchmarking competitors will help the development of ideas. Multiple interviews with high-producing targets, including developing focus groups, should be a part of the development phase. Even when an idea is developed, the rapidly changing market is likely to alter their needs as rapidly as the salesperson is able to deliver the value.

If you get the impression that developing value-added programs is a major commitment—you are correct. The professional is one who recognizes the significance of these goals in the overall success strategy, and will there for dedicate the necessary energy toward develop these value-added programs. Meanwhile, the traditional salesperson is attempting to make a sale one day at a time.

A professional realizes it is more than just dressing. Ever since the *Dress For Success* phenomenon swept America many years ago, business people have been more cognizant of the effect of appearance upon results. Once again, America has moved in another direction and *business casual* is all the rage as many companies are disdaining suits and ties for business casual attire. Success never was dictated through $1,500 suits and $500 loafers. On the other hand, unprofessional dress—casual or not—will certainly be a deterrent to any form of success. Many in the world of business go calling in garb that is barely acceptable for Sunday afternoon football, let alone to impress someone. True professionals may actually dress up or down, depending upon the traits exhibited by the target. Either way, they are professionally appointed—and realize that there is more to professionalism than what is on the outside.

A professional shows it through their behavior and communication. Are your words and actions expressed through a professional demeanor? Do you become unglued in pressure situations, within the office and/or on the road? Is your language appropriate for the situations for which it is utilized? And by language, we do not just mean vulgar expressions. By examining your speech patterns you may find reflections that do not spell success in any way, shape or fashion. Observe the difference between a polished professional and one of the masses. Compare a leader making an eloquent speech to 200 industry leaders with the next time you are the recipient of a stumbling cold call. A leader communicates in such a way that exudes confidence and inspiration.

A professional is organized. Ask any business person for a self-improvement itinerary and better organizational skills will top most lists. Desired by all and achieved by few, too many of us exhibit unprofessional behavior by wasting time looking for data that should be easily attainable in our filing systems. There are many ways our customers will be exposed to our unprofessional organizational skills:

◆ Our response time is hampered by never being able to *put a finger* directly upon the information;

◆ We may be late for appointments and in our timing of follow-up;

◆ We are disoriented at times we should be exhibiting traits of decisiveness; and,

◆ We also waste valuable time being disorganized and influence our support staff to do the same.

A professional has the attitude. While everyone has an attitude, a professional's attitude spells success. William James, a 20th century philosopher said:

> *"The greatest discovery of my generation is that human beings can alter their lives by altering their mental attitudes."*

Henry Ford said:

> *"If you think you can, you will.*
> *If you think you can't, you won't."*

No one succeeds without an attitude that says simply:

> *"Yes I can and yes I will."*

Those without this attitude will be halted by the obstacles we face every day: changes in market conditions, pricing competition, limited resources and even a lack of vision. We see it every day in Pareto's principle in that every sales force has a limited number of those who are exceedingly successful. And then there are the masses. The only difference? Attitude, attitude, and attitude.

It is this attitude that leads us to organize and implement our plan. It helps us realize that we must work hard and conduct ourselves professionally to succeed. Realizing that these conditions must prevail is one thing, carrying them out is something else. A positive attitude carries us through the obstacles that lie before us—Must start the day at 5:00 in the morning to get ahead? A must do attitude makes it happen. Have to block out negative attitudes that prevail all around you? A positive attitude provides the necessary focus.

It is attitude that facilitates the achievements of the other traits essential to being of a professional. With regard to ethics, it is a professional attitude that enables one to be honest with oneself. For example, do you have the knowledge necessary to succeed in tomorrow's world? Knowledge of your own company and industry, your competitors, technology and your targets. Those who are honest recognize their shortcomings and are continually attempting to increase their knowledge component. The attainment of knowledge becomes a specific goal and part of the vision. Those without the attitude feel that increasing their knowledge level will not help them with immediate tasks, therefore the goal of increasing their knowledge level does not become part of their long-range plan.

It is attitude that is the deciding factor in enabling us to become a professional. In the coming years, the world of business success will be dominated more and more by those who are dedicated to the level of professionalism necessary to conquer a new world again and again. The traditional salesperson, existing in his/her own small space and focusing on the specific task that lies in their immediate path is likely to become a dinosaur as we move forward within the 21st Century.

If you truly want more productivity with less stress you must put yourself in a position to implement the rules of synergy. To put yourself in a position, you must demonstrate these traits of success. From attitude to professionalism and back to attitude. Fortunately, the choice of paths is yours.

CHAPTER THREE
The Application of Maximum Synergy Through a Comprehensive Marketing Plan

"An aim in life is the only fortune worth finding."
Jacqueline Kennedy Onassis

If you are truly interested in increasing your income, then you must start at the beginning with a *marketing plan*. If you are missing a marketing plan you will be without a blueprint for success. You may not even recognize success when you are close because you have not defined success in your own terms. Our maximum synergy rules will help obtain more from our resources but without the marketing plan we may not be able to take full advantage of this effectiveness because we will not know if we are moving in the right direction at all times.

Marketing plan components

There are four key components of a marketing plan:

- ◆ *Action*—Each marketing plan will have several actions that are designed to provide **diversity** to the plan. Each action should be responsible for a certain percent of your total income and this will be specified within your *goal statement.*
- ◆ *Target*—Each action has a defined *target group* that is to be reached with a marketing tool. The *target groups* and *marketing tools* are defined to provide *specialization* and linked to provide *diversity.*
- ◆ *Frequency*—The frequency of the actions is defined to create *consistency.*
- ◆ *Evaluation*—The evaluation results in adjustment of actions, targets, frequencies and tools so that the original goals are achieved during changing conditions.

We will be addressing each of these components individually at different stages within this chapter and further within the following chapters focusing upon marketing and sales tools, but before moving to the specific components, it is important to examine some of the concepts upon which the success of the marketing plan is predicated.

Why diversify?

Before you begin to set your goals, you must decide from where your business is going to originate. It should not be difficult to understand the importance of diversification of your marketing plan. Diversification is a basic tenet of any business, yet every time the market changes the majority of businesses become victimized by making adjustments too slowly. A salesperson or business owner should be no different than a major corporation that seeks to be stronger through diversity. If your business plan is to succeed, it must succeed through changing markets. Change is the one constant we can depend upon each year. It seems that every year we say that there has been none other like the present.

When one seeks to diversify, we must recognize that there are several areas that we will have to address. Diversity means more than increasing business sources. There are several ways to diversify:

◆ Marketing tools
◆ Price Ranges
◆ Geographics
◆ Demographics
◆ Delivery methods

The tools of the plan

If we were carpenters, it would not be hard to identify our tools. Sales professionals utilize tools constantly without recognizing what they are. Consequently, their tools may not be used in their most effective fashion. What are some common tools of business?

◆ Letters
◆ Direct mail lists
◆ The telephone
◆ The media
◆ Business cards
◆ Name tags

- Signs
- Flyers
- Presentations
- E-mail
- Websites
- Computers

This list of tools could go on and on, but the point is well taken. If you do not think of the telephone as a sales tool, you are not likely to utilize it in such a way that it can become an integral part of your marketing plan. As a matter of fact, the misuse of a tool such as a telephone can actually cost you potential sales via the facets of the plan designed to generate business.

Maximum synergy requires the judicious choice of the most effective tools. You very well might use more than one tool to reach a target group. Conversely, you might also try to reach more than one group with the utilization of one tool or through one action.

The targets of business

Before one can begin to identify actions that will help us meet the goals of our marketing plan, we must first identify the targets of our approach. This is very important because without proper identification of our targets, we will become part of the mass of professionals who deploy a *scatter-gun* approach to sales. For your marketing efforts to be successful, you must know your target well:

- Demographics: age, sex, education and other characteristics.
- Geographics: boundaries and the characteristics of a defined area.
- Use of product: for example, investment or consumption.
- Corporations, consumers or professional groups.

We can go on and on with our list. It is important to be as exhaustive as possible because our list of targets can be our base of ideas for actions and opportunities for synergies that emanate from these actions. For example, a Realtor® might propose a seminar on the merits of investing in real estate and present this seminar with their secondary target—financial planners. The primary target for both actors would be real estate investors.

It is also important to recognize that our advice to maintain your strength by becoming diversified should not be taken as guidance to target everyone. No plan can be effective if your target is the whole world. By the same token, the concept of diversity also allows for the professional to become specialized—specialized, yes; totally dependent, no.

Ready, set, action!

All the planning in the world will not substitute for the most important component: action. When we analyze the top traits of professionals, we concluded that desire and attitude are keys to success. This is no surprise. There are those who will plan all day. There are others who will take action.

It is our suggestion that your actions be developed in such a way that they will create synergy (effectiveness), continue over the long term (consistency), and happen with great frequency (persistency). Synergy, consistency and frequency are the keys to the success of any action plan. It is only those who are willing to pay the price for success who will actually succeed.

The actions will actually combine the tools and targets we have identified in our plan. The following would be a sample action plan statement:

"Mail newsletters (350) to ABC one time per quarter"

This statement is actually missing some very important components. We have not identified the desired results (goals) and have not identified specifically how the newsletters are going to help us reach those goals. Are we looking for referrals or new purchases? How can we use the concept of synergy to achieve more than one goal at once?

Evaluation

The final stage of implementing any marketing plan is the evaluation of the results. Having definitive goals enables us to measure the results of our actions and make decisions regarding changes that must be effected. A marketing plan is not a stagnant document. All parts of the plan, from targets to tools to activities, must be changed when necessary so that we are always moving closer to the achievement of our goals. Without this change, our plan will not be constantly moving us consistently in the right direction. In today's world characterized by constant and rapid change, these adjustments are imperative.

Goals represent the starting point

The process of goal planning should first begin by deciding what is important to us. Day by day we seem to get lost in the challenges of daily life. It is hard to think of the long term when we are stuck in traffic and we can't get to our next appointment. It is hard to think of saving for retirement when we are trying to make the next mortgage payment. Isn't this an opportune time to ask at what juncture we will address the significant things in life?

So what is important?

Health. There is nothing more important than one's health. Today, medical advances have made a longer life possible for the average citizen. For those who do not take advantage of today's advanced medical techniques and knowledge, a longer and healthier life is not ensured. What can you do to be healthier? The rules are easy—stop smoking, exercise regularly, eat sensibly and see your doctor on a regular basis. As easy as these rules are, how many make resolutions each year to do one or more of these things and then never follow through?

Lower Stress Levels. Doesn't it seem as though each year we have more and more time-saving devices, yet less time? More significantly, each device that allows us to be in constant contact with the business world—from cell phones to wireless modems—makes it harder and harder for us to just *get away from it all.* Many of us return from long weekends without piles of phone messages. That is the good news. The bad news is that we are answering e-mail while we are away and supposed to be relaxing.

So how do we reduce stress? Take some time every day to refresh and recharge our batteries. It does not have to be hours—it can be minutes. Clear away the thousands of thoughts and just think about being relaxed. Get a massage. And here is the good news—less stress means a healthier life!

Move Towards Financial Security. Want less stress in your life? Have a financial plan that is helping you move towards your long-term financial goals. It is never too late to begin a savings plan. Take advantage of your company's 401K or other tax deductible retirement savings plan. If you have children, are you putting money away for their college education? If you have an investment portfolio, is it being reviewed for long-term objectives such as diversification and protection against inflation?

Make Your Career More Rewarding. Before you determine your annual goals, determine what will make you a success in your eyes. Is it earning enough income to provide a secure future for your family? Is it advancing within your company? Is it starting your own company and being your own boss?

Nothing is more stressful than working hard every year and feeling that you never *get ahead.* First you must determine what *getting ahead* means to you. Then you must take the steps necessary that move you in the right direction.

Perhaps it is adding skills such as computer programming. Or perhaps it is additional sales training.

Now that you have identified your goals move towards achieving them . . .

Look at the long term. It has been said that if you don't know where you are going, how do you know when you have arrived? Too many of us get up every day and work dutifully in a direction of which we are sure will lead to long-term happiness. On the other hand, most of us have not defined these long-term goals.

One word of caution—do not expect the act of meeting long-term goals to bring you happiness. People do not become happy because they retire, they are happy because they are at peace with their situation. If you are presently unhappy, you must recognize that you are the only one who can improve your outlook. It is a question of a wealthy attitude, not material wealth.

Achieve a little of your goals each day. Rome was not built in a day. Nor will you reach your long-term goals in a few weeks, months or even in a short year. The important thing is to move a little closer to your goal each day. Remember those "things to do lists" you were advised to fill out each and every day by time management experts? Which items on your list are the most important with regard to long-term goal achievement? Prioritize these each and every day.

Your goals should be measurable. Significant goals such as happiness, security and prestige sound great on paper—but how do you know how close you are to these objectives? You must have a system of measurement so that you can determine your standards of achievement. Security might denote the ability to leave your job any time you wish. How much money in the bank brings to you this definition of security?

Make sure your goals are realistic but out of your reach. In the short term, your goals must make you reach or you will never move forward. Put these objectives too far out of reach and they will never motivate you to move towards them at all. If your goal is to achieve a $100,000 in annual income and your last calendar year brought earnings of $30,000, what are the chances of achieving your goal within six months?

There is a greater chance that you can move to $50,000 one year and $75,000 the next. Doesn't seem like much of an achievement when you are aiming higher? How many workers more than double their income in two years?

Tell the world. Do not keep your goals to yourself. Inform your employer, peers, spouse and your targets. Do this for two reasons. First, making your goals public makes it more likely that you will commit to achieving your objectives. Second, achieving significant objectives is a much more difficult task when you are working alone. Your best customers become advocates when they become a part of your marketing plan. This will give you many chances to invoke the laws of synergy. Your spouse can provide motivation every day. Your employer may be able to allocate resources towards the quest. Working alone may seem like a proud thing to accomplish, but it is not very efficient.

Short-term action goals are the key to achieving long-term results

Many of us will relate to our short-term goals more easily than the longer-term objectives because short-term goals deal with our every day actions. Most people in business compile a daily *to do list* or undergo some form of weekly or monthly planning. We recognize these actions as appointments, phone calls, cold calls, filing, reading, reports, sales meetings, training classes and a host of other daily business renderings.

It is the implementation of these everyday actions that determine whether we will meet our broader objectives. We effect these actions to meet some sort of goal:

*Make ten calls to previous prospects each
day to set up three appointments*

Most of us have not gone the extra step to provide linkage of these actions to effect our ultimate goals and objectives. It is one thing to equate more calls to greater sales, it is another to follow through by linking the action to the real desired results:

*Make ten calls to previous prospects each day to
set up three appointments resulting in one new relationship
each week accounting for a 20 percent increase in income
annually. Eight percent of this increase is earmarked for a
savings plan that will move up the planned retirement
date by a total of six years.*

It is this linkage that will make all the difference in the world. Short-term actions will mean little unless we know where they are taking us. Long-term goals mean little if there are no individual actions to get us there. Together, we will know our destination and how we are going to arrive.

Target identification is key

*"Competition brings out the best in products
and the worst in people."*
David Sarnoff

For many, it is the selection of the correct targets that will determine the overall effectiveness of our marketing plans. Many of us take our targets for granted because they are easily identified:

◆ If we are real estate agents, our target may be the home buying public or businesses;

◆ If we are mortgage loan officers, our targets may be real estate agents or direct consumers;

◆ If we are casualty insurance agents, our targets may be owners of office buildings;

◆ If we are pension fund managers, our targets may be the human resources departments of larger employers; and,

◆ If we are selling advertising for a teen magazine, our targets would be companies who design products that appeal to the demographic profile of our publication.

The correct identification of targets is very important in three respects: marketing efficiency, specialization and diversification. These three concepts comprise the reasons why target analysis is imperative before we develop a definitive marketing plan. Without the careful analysis of our proposed targets from a standpoint of how their selection can affect achievement of our long-term objectives, we may be directing our efforts in the wrong direction.

Marketing efficiency

Take the example of a real estate agent. The home-buying public is a rather large target group. This is good because there exists great numbers of them across our country. The group is as large and diverse as the United States— actually too large and too diverse to be of help in any systematic marketing effort (over two-thirds of American families own homes). Going after every potential homebuyer would certainly require quite a large marketing effort. In the long run, we can break larger targets down into more manageable segments, enabling us to identify more specific target groups for which we can set up a definitive marketing strategy:

◆ homebuyers who are purchasing their first home;

◆ homebuyers in a certain geographic area or subdivision;

- buyers of a certain type of home, such as condominiums;
- homebuyers who have a home to sell (move-up buyers);
- homebuyers who are relocating into a specific area;
- homebuyers who are relocating out of a specific area;
- homebuyers who are in a certain price range or economic strata;
- homebuyers who work for a particular employer(s);
- homebuyers who are of a certain immigrant or ethnic group;
- homebuyers who have recently graduated from college;
- homebuyers who are recently married;
- homebuyers who are recently divorced;
- homebuyers who are purchasing vacation property;
- homebuyers who are purchasing rental (investment) property; and,
- homebuyers who are looking for retirement homes.

You can see how each of these smaller target groups lend themselves to a more specific marketing effort. Our geographic and demographic identification of market segments will enable us to tailor our marketing efforts to a particular group within a particular area. Without the identification of specific targets within the home-buying public, any marketing effort will be fraught with inefficiencies. Only a scatter-gun approach can reach the general public. Such an approach is expensive and only companies national in scope can afford to blanket the general public with advertising. Individuals and the vast majority of American companies have to be more judicious with their marketing resources. We need to receive a maximum response for every dollar or effort we expend. In today's competitive environment, no business entity can afford wasted resources, especially those that are as precious as time and money.

Specialization

When we go through the process of target identification for the purpose of marketing efficiency, another opportunity arises. At this juncture, we can now identify possible market niches that will make us a specialist within our field. Though a specialty is not required for success in business, it does give one several advantages in the pursuit of greater achievement.

It gives us the opportunity to be known as an expert as compared to the competition that is trying to equally serve all possible targets:

> *"John is the one to deal with if you are purchasing
> a condominium in this area."*

In this example, the real estate agent has positioned himself in the minds of the target audience. He has elevated himself among his peers to a level of expertise and now has a marked advantage versus those with whom he is competing.

It enables us to concentrate our marketing resources within a specific area and thus generate a higher rate of return on our marketing dollars and make it possible for us to dominate our competition:

"Mary has that subdivision locked-up because she is so entrenched through her concentrated efforts over the years."

In the above case, the real estate agent may be on the board of directors of the homeowners association, have sponsored community events, written the neighborhood newsletter, etc. She has become an integral part of the community. It is unlikely that her competition could expend the energy to match her concentrated efforts because this type of domination requires long-term, focused energy that may have a limited rate of return in the short run.

Our familiarity with the scope of the target will enable us to take advantage of all business opportunities available. A cursory treatment of a particular target may show us one opportunity to make sales:

"Mark regularly direct mails to the Greentree Condominium to solicit for listings in that community."

There is no doubt about the fact that Mark may be successful in reaching potential sellers through his direct mail effort. If this is one of many efforts directed towards many targets, it is unlikely that he would be able to see and/or take advantage of the following opportunities that exist within the same complex (synergy rules require that his eyes open a little wider):

◆ purchasers moving into the complex;
◆ those renting in the complex who might purchase here or elsewhere;
◆ those who own in the complex, but rent the units (investors in real estate); and,
◆ move-up buyers moving out of the complex.

It may be more efficient to take advantage of the potential sales from this one target rather than looking elsewhere for additional sources of business. We would reach these additional sources with less resources (and less stress) because our energies are already focused among these targets. Target specialization enables us to increase our efficiency within the target group and within groups that are ancillary to the primary target. It is at this juncture that the concept of target diversity comes in to play.

Target diversity

As we mentioned in our introduction of this chapter, it may seem to be a conflict to be reaching for target *specialization* on one hand and *diversity* on the other. However, the two concepts are not in any way mutually exclusive. It is our comprehensive treatment of targets that enables us to uncover opportunities to *become diverse* by linking our efforts. If all of our marketing efforts are not linked, any effort to become diversified will be inefficient. Going back to our example of the condominium complex, the real estate agent may recognize the opportunity to service more than one target:

- the condominium complex;
- financial planners who refer potential purchasers of investment property;
- the human resources department of a nearby employer.

Without any linkage between these targets, each effort will have to be carried independently without any mutual benefit. In other words, they are merely multiple sources of business. On the other hand, linkage gives us the ability to take advantage of major synergistic opportunities. Now let's take a look at these targets a little more closely:

Condominium	Financial Planners	Human Resources
Sellers within the complex;	Purchasers of larger homes;	Higher-level management
Purchasers who are now renting in the complex;	Purchasers of investment real estate;	Employees relocating into the area
Investors who might purchase units within the complex;	Sellers of present homes (move-up); and,	Employees who are currently renting
Purchasers from outside the complex;	Those who may be gifting money to their children to purchase real estate	Current owners within the complex who are employees of the company
Investors who might sell to their present renters; and,		
Move-up buyers who are selling their units		

In this case, you can see a definite linkage between investors who might purchase units in the complex (under condominium) and purchasers of investment real estate (under financial planners and higher-level management). It is this linkage that might be your basis for developing relationships with financial planners—after all, you are the expert dealing with a potential investment (the condominium). This contributes to your target diversification efforts.

Your linkage between investors (financial planners) and the investment (condominiums) will not at all preclude you from taking advantage of the other needs of the financial planners' client (for example, move-up purchases). This will be a natural extension of your business and your plan automatically becomes diversified by establishment of the first specific linkage. More importantly, the diversity comes with efforts reinforcing the effectiveness of other marketing efforts. You will see, as you develop your overall marketing plan, the establishment of links between targets and marketing efforts is the key to the successful evolution of an effective and efficient plan. This illustrated concept represents a significant example of how the application of synergy rules can help you achieve more with less resources:

- ◆ Linkage of targets makes it easier to achieve more than one objective with the same action;
- ◆ The selection of linked targets prove that these targets are more effective than others; and,
- ◆ Additional doses of synergy can be added to one area of your marketing plan, rather than marketing in many different directions.

Creating value for your targets

The development of a linkage between your targets is not enough to ensure the success of a marketing plan. Maximum synergy comes from providing more than a good product and/or service to your targets. Maximum synergy comes from adding value to their personal or business existence. The linkage of your targets should be designed to accomplish more than diversity and efficiency. The targets should be related in such a way that they can help you bring value to the table. Becoming a target specialist facilitates the identification and delivery of value within your marketing plan.

Let us return to the example of linkage between the financial planner, residents of a condominium and the human resources department of a local employer. How can these targets be linked so that you can provide more value?

- You can do a joint mailing with the financial planner. Mailing articles on the topics of investing, savings plans, etc. would help increase the client base for the financial planner. Providing the articles to the residents of the complex or the employees of the local company adds value to their lives.

- You can hold a joint home-buyers seminar with the financial planner. These seminars could be held in the community center of the condominium complex or the conference room of the employer. The added value would be similar to what is achieved by mailing articles regularly.

- You can refer your customers to this financial planner when there is a need. For example, many homeowners will ask about additional life insurance after they purchase a home. They may want to make sure that the mortgage is taken care of in the event of their death. Providing the name of a reliable financial planner provides extra value to your customer.

You can see why a relationship in which you are asking for referrals from financial planners and there is no reciprocation will not work in the long run. This target must be provided with value in return. As they begin to recognize the value they are receiving, they will work hard to return value in your direction (the law of reciprocity).

It is the provision of value that allows us to separate ourselves from our competitors in the long run. There is no better way to solidify our standing with our targets than to add real value to their lives. The efficiencies of our marketing efforts will multiply many times after we add this important component into our design and implementation.

The tools of the plan

> *"Ben Franklin may have discovered electricity, but it is*
> *the guy who invented the meter who made all the money."*
> Gerald Ronald Yates

If we don't match the correct tool to reach our targets, the vast majority of marketing efforts will become less effective. Additionally, if we don't identify the broad range of tools available, it is unlikely we will be in a position to choose the most efficient alternatives to reach our targets.

The identification of the tools available to us is quite a task for most industries because there are so many possibilities. Let's take a look at a few of the more common tools used to reach targets of the business world.

General advertising:

- ◆ Television
- ◆ Radio
- ◆ Print
- ◆ Signs and billboards
- ◆ The Internet

Targeted advertising

- ◆ Direct mail
- ◆ Newsletters
- ◆ Brochures
- ◆ Industry specific periodicals
- ◆ Telemarketing

Direct individual contact

- ◆ Telephone
- ◆ Appointments
- ◆ Networking
- ◆ Lunches
- ◆ Business cards

Each of these categories is comprised of more specific tools that further define our options. Let's look at an example illustrating this concept:

The financial planner decides to increase business by utilizing a networking approach.

- ◆ The planner may decide to start/join *networking groups* that are comprised of professionals from different industries. These groups have regular *meetings* in which business cards and ideas are exchanged.
- ◆ The planner may utilize his/her own personal contacts to join organizations to start networking. These organizations might include their church or temple, the PTA, a country club membership board, etc. The planner might attend *meetings*, hand

out *business cards* and garner the names of prospects (*referrals*) that are members of these organizations.

◆ The planner may decide to *telephone* professional contacts to garner *referrals* (either over the phone or through a follow-up *meeting*). These professional contacts would constitute the base of the networking efforts.

◆ The planner may utilize a *computer* with *contact management software* to organize and facilitate the networking effort. In today's world of automation, business people can procure programs that will schedule *calls*, dial the *phone* and *fax* follow-up documents. Further, the same computer might send *e-mail* messages over the *Internet* to start a networking group on-line.

◆ The planner may conduct a *direct mail* campaign to present customers, offering a free product or service (*promotion*) as an enticement for referrals.

◆ The planner may simply give out three *business cards* and ask for *referrals* from everyone he/she is in contact with on a daily basis.

It is clear that the financial planner must know the tools available before making a correct decision on the direction of the marketing plan. If the planner does not know about the existence of networking groups, then he/she is likely to use more limited resources to establish the network. This would be a major disadvantage if the person had limited personal and professional contacts—a probable characteristic of someone new to the industry or business in general. If the planner is not well versed regarding the potential of automation, it is unlikely that maximum efficiencies will be reached in the long run even if the networking groups are utilized.

Take note of what is lurking under your nose

Many times we as business people elect to utilize a particular tool because it is an industry standard or because it is the easiest to identify and utilize (or so we think). In the case of the financial planner, marketing can be accomplished over the telephone. It is likely that the financial planner who utilizes the phone regularly will see the phone as a major marketing tool. On the other hand, a planner who spends most of his/her time on the road in face-to-face contact may see the phone as a hindrance rather than a tool:

"I can't get on the road to sell because I can't get off the phone."

It is a fact that the way we view tools will affect whether they become an integral part of our marketing plan or whether they become an obstruction to plan implementation. If the person sees the phone as a hindrance he/she may actually prevent a future sale or lose a present customer while they are hurrying to get on the road.

In this regard, the development of skills in order to better utilize a particular marketing instrument can become a goal within itself. In the era of the rapid development of automation, how many of us have made it a goal to better employ the use of a computer or particular software application? Knowing that a tool exists is not enough to contribute to our success. We must be able to manipulate the tool in such a way that it is helping us achieve the maximum capacity that can result from that instrument.

In many cases, knowing how to utilize the tool is not the problem. Sometimes we overlook the ability of the tool to assist us in our efforts. For example, if you are on the road constantly, one tool we may overlook is the cell phone. Many of us utilize cells for returning calls and phone emergencies. If you are in the car for at least 60 minutes each day, the cell phone can be an integral part of your marketing plan. Simply schedule to make a certain number of marketing calls each day from the car instead of reacting to calls you are receiving. *If you make five extra marketing calls each day, this amounts to 1,000 to 1,250 each year.* (Note: be sure to use hands free option for safety.)

This plan may result in a significant increase in your marketing capacity without any increase in time expended. Remember that time is a person's most valuable asset, therefor a more efficient utilization of your time will result in an increase in overall marketing efficiency. Synergy dictates that we accomplish more with our everyday actions.

Make sure you link your tools

Many times we use several marketing tools without developing a linkage within our overall marketing plan. The independence of any facet of our marketing plan may very well produce general marketing inefficiencies. Let's take another example:

The financial planner is using the following tools:

- ◆ direct print advertising in a local newspaper; and,
- ◆ writing a newsletter on investment/retirement strategies—
  directly mailed to his/her customer base.

Many local newspapers have a dearth of writers on many subjects. They pay for syndicated columnists to provide interesting articles on housing, finance, political opinions, etc. If the planner is already writing interesting articles and is presently an advertising customer of the paper, why not approach the paper to publish articles from the newsletter? These would be interesting to the readership base of the newspaper and also would represent free publicity/marketing to the planner. In addition, if the planner is placing an ad in the newspaper, why not offer a free copy of the newsletter as a response mechanism?

Don't overlook the most important marketing tool—yourself

We can concoct the most elaborate marketing system with the most advanced tools possible, yet, the success of our mission will still be limited by the most important variable in the equation—ourselves! We can direct mail, telephone, visit or drop an atomic bomb—if the messenger is not first rate all efforts will be for naught. We have covered this topic in detail in Chapter Two of this book focusing on traits. These traits are limiting factors. This means that without these traits all marketing dollars/efforts will be wasted.

Diversification is essential for long-term success

As we have said, our call for business diversification within our description of the importance of the marketing plan may well sound like conflicting advice if one pays attention to our call in another section for a specific, focused plan. While it is true that finding our market niche is very important, that niche can actually lead to increased diversification of our efforts. The process of diversifying involves the linkage of tools, targets and strategies in such a way that synergy can be created. If we do not specifically identify these tools, targets and strategies, the process of diversification will more resemble an attempt of trial and error and, in effect, we will be trying to be all things to all targets.

It is just as important for a small business or salesperson to have a diversified marketing plan as it is for a major corporation. Any business that is too dependent upon one source of business or tool for business development will be susceptible to vacillating business cycles. Do you ever wonder why some businesses do well through recessions while others struggle? Diversity can mean insulation. While we desire our target to be very specific, we may want our attack on that target to come from many directions.

The process of diversification can affect many aspects of our business plan. Here are a few examples of how our diversification can be achieved:

◆ selling more than one product to the same target;
◆ selling one product to more than one target;

◆ using more than one source to reach the same target; and,

◆ using several points of contact to introduce your company/product to a new target.

None of these examples of diversification should come as a surprise or are difficult to identify. It is usually difficult to limit your focus to a few targets, products and tools and be consistent in the pursuit of these. However, even more difficult is the use of synergy to link these in a way that the business can diversify without significantly increasing the use of monetary resources and/or time.

For example, let us say we are selling financial products such as life insurance. We may decide that an effective synergy marketing partner would be certified public accountants (CPAs)—because accountants give tax advice that may affect the decision as to what type and amount of life insurance may be advisable within a long-term financial plan.

We are also cognizant of the fact that we must continually market our present customer base to procure the sales of additional products and referrals. Within the diversification process, we may decide to use our contact with our present customer base to procure referrals to accountants already serving our present customers. This would enable us to make contact with our present clients (an important strategy) with the dual goal of being able to increase sales and strengthen our relationship with them while we diversify towards another effective target. Maximum synergy rule number three indicates that some targets are more effective than others. In this case, we have surveyed one effective target (previous customers) and move to the objective of diversification through linkage to another effective target (CPAs).

Evaluation

All the planning and hard work of sales will never come to fruition unless we stop to *smell the roses* periodically. In this context, we mean more than pausing to enjoy our successes. We also mean setting up a process by which we evaluate constantly whether our daily actions are helping us achieve our success goals.

Too often we spend New Year's Day evaluating the year behind us. *Where did the time go? Why don't I feel as though I accomplished anything?* While it is never a bad idea to reflect upon the year, it is not likely that we can correct a plan gone astray in a few hours after we have moved in a certain direction for 365 days. Evaluation must be a constant part of every marketing plan.

Goals come first

As we have stated continuously, we must start with the identification of goals. It makes sense that before we evaluate we must first make sure that we have definitive standards by which we are going to measure success. We can divide our goals into three components:

Long-term goals are those that define our success standards during our lifetime. These would involve personal, social, family, economic and professional goals. Many times these goals are viewed as being interconnected. For example, our economic goals may very well be defined in terms of future security for the family. To identify these goals you must ask yourself:

- ◆ What do I want to accomplish in life?
- ◆ When do I want to retire and with what standards?
- ◆ How do I want my family to grow?

Intermediate goals are those that you may reflect upon on New Year's Day. If your long-term goal is retirement, was your annual income of a level to move toward that goal? If your goal is a college education for the children, did you put money away and was their academic progress commensurate with these goals?

Short-term goals are often overlooked because they are hard to see from the forest of every day life. Annual income is easy to measure. The causal/effect relationship between the activities of one day (or an hour) and the year are less clear. If you often feel disappointed with the day, but feel that you can always *make it up tomorrow*, this does not bode well with regard to achieving your long-term goals.

Our short-term goals are as specific as every activity we undertake. Unless every marketing activity has a goal, we cannot evaluate whether that activity will help us in the long run. This means a goal for *every* action:

- ◆ If you effect a mailing, what is your expected response rate?
- ◆ If you take five lead calls, how many of these do you expect to convert into transactions?
- ◆ If you make a sales call, when is your goal to be writing a contract?
- ◆ When you attend a sales seminar, what do you expect to modify in your plan?
- ◆ What do you expect to accomplish today with regard to your overall marketing plan?

◆ What do you expect to accomplish tomorrow and the next day?

The example of taking a potential homebuyer to look at homes should serve us well. Steve Stewart, a noted real estate trainer, says it well in the title of his seminar: *Buy From Me Or Get Out Of My Car*. As humorous as that sounds, the point is well taken. If someone is *just looking* you are not likely to achieve the goal of selling a home. As a matter of fact, the time you waste with a person *just looking* will prevent you from selling a home to a legitimate buyer.

This sounds crazy to most sales professionals who reason—*"I am not taking anyone else out today, and maybe they will buy eventually."* It seems that the activity is filling a need of being busy. If your goal is fulfillment of the need to be a tour guide, then go ahead. If your goal is to sell homes, evaluate. How many hours will you allocate to these people before you move on? When you return home did you put yourself in a position to write a contract? If not, ask the people some probing questions:

Did we accomplish what you expected?

What is your time frame for purchasing?

What home will motivate you to write?

If you are afraid to ask these questions for fear of being too pushy or turning people off, you may be as afraid of success as you are of failure. If their answer is—*we are just looking and do not want to purchase this year*—mail them nice pictures periodically and see them next year. Keep in touch so that they do not use another agent (or better yet, if they want to continue to shop—refer them to one). And . . . ask them if they know someone who wants to buy now.

For many, the process of evaluation, if accomplished correctly, will cause them to make major changes in their marketing efforts. When we evaluate, we must be prepared to put everything on the table—our targets, tools, activities and overall objectives. We return to that important quote—*The true definition of insanity is doing the same thing over and over and expecting a different result.* If your evaluation process leads to no significant changes, you are not likely to alter your results.

CHAPTER FOUR
The Sales Skills and Tools Necessary to Effect Maximum Synergy

"Success consists of getting up just one more time than you fall."
Ralph Waldo Emerson

We can plan to effect the best marketing actions in the world. We can generate hundreds of fully qualified leads with a minimum of resources. But this planning and effort will all be for naught unless we can convert these leads to actual sales. We have actually introduced some of the most important sales skills needed to implement our synergy rules during our discussion of the necessary traits. For example, great sales skills include asking for the business and overcoming call reluctance.

However, it is one thing to state that a successful salesperson must ask for the business and another thing to help one achieve that goal. Everyone knows they are supposed to ask and yet few do. In other words, the solutions are a bit more complex than the problems as simply stated.

In this chapter, we will introduce several sales skills and follow with a more in-depth discussion of areas where one may find solutions to age-old sales issues. Like the traits, these skills are a limiting factor. As they say in lottery advertising: *You can't win if you don't play.* If you don't go through the sales process, you will not succeed. Period.

Call reluctance—if you don't call you can't ask

We will discuss the facets of call reluctance in the context of analyzing many aspects of the sales process. Reluctance not only keeps us from making calls, it keeps us from asking and closing within the process of effecting sales calls.

There are many types of call reluctance, from the "over-preparer" to those who will not call upon high-level targets or CEOs (socially self-conscious). It is important to note that everyone possesses some form of call reluctance. If you are interested in learning more about the types of call reluctance refer to works such as *Earning What You're Worth? The Psychology of Sales Call Reluctance* (Dudley, Goodson and Barnett Behavior Sciences Research Press, 1995 edition).

Top producers tend to conquer their reticence easier while those who fail are consumed by these same feelings. In other words, everyone would benefit by recognizing in which cases they are likely to shy away from taking an important sales action and then applying an important psychological fix that we will call—

Get over it!

Yes, there is no more important action one needs to do than *get over it*. It may not be as easy as it sounds, but if we have a hard time asking, we need to *get over it* and ask. In the real world, we are sure that most salespeople would just do it on their own if they could, so it is important for us to offer solutions in the form of actions we can take to help us *get over it* by.

- ◆ delivering more value up-front (synergy rule number seven), we are more likely to ask for the business.
- ◆ setting specific goals for certain activities (for example calls to previous customers) and monitoring results on a daily basis.
- ◆ scheduling activities that we are likely to overlook if they are not specifically on our calendar.
- ◆ eliminating obstacles that are being used as excuses for keeping us from doing what we need to do.
- ◆ identifying and isolating the sources of our reluctance. Is it reluctance to use the phone or reluctance to make calls face-to-face? You cannot overcome reluctance unless you know specifically what must be attacked.
- ◆ pairing up with "buddies" or "coaches" who will give us daily encouragement to take certain actions (synergy partners, for example).
- ◆ making it fun. Contests, challenges and games may be seen as "infantile" by some, but they are really major sales tools. In reality, if we do not like what we are doing, we are less likely to accomplish the task.
- ◆ being honest with ourselves. If we are going to overcome an obstacle we must admit that our own call reluctance (and attitude) is the problem, not all the other things we have been blaming— such as paperwork and the competition.

We must first recognize the problem before we can attack it. Knowing that we have call reluctance is half the battle, but we cannot win the battle without a specific plan. Motivational seminars and books may lift our spirits for short periods of time, but nothing substitutes for actual planning and execution. If you want to be motivated, try taking an action that is different and witness a different (and better) result. Nothing motivates more than success. If we are going to *get over it,* we need to understand and experience what results we can achieve with a little less reluctance.

Cold calling—sometimes you must

When you read the chapter of this book focusing upon marketing tools, you will get the impression that we do not think highly of the activity of "cold calling." Businesses actually ignore previous and present customers as sources of additional business while they spend their time focusing upon cold calling for new business. We spend much time and resources bringing in this business and our easiest source of additional business is our existing relationships. Yet, bookstores are filled with works teaching us how to become effective cold callers through advanced solicitation techniques. One excellent such work is *Red-Hot Cold Call Selling* (Goldner, American Management Association, 1995).

In fact, there are some situations in which salespeople and business owners are going to be expected to be able to cold call. For example, telemarketers are many times put in the position to be cold call experts. If you are moving into a new sales position in a new geographic area and/or are selling a new product, you may not have a base of existing business or relationships from which to build. Also, you may be selling within a very specific business niche that requires new contacts be initiated. So in deference to our own advice, we are going to present a few tips for cold calling.

- ◆ *Address your problems with call reluctance up-front.* If you are consumed with call reluctance, cold calling may not be for you. On the other hand, there are those who are reluctant to call upon those with whom they have a close relationship and may prefer cold calling. In most situations salespeople will be more effective utilizing those relationships as a basis for their calls—and we stick with this advice even as we move to help our readers be more effective calling sources with whom they have no relationship. The bottom line: whether you are cold calling or networking, if you do not prospect your sources, you will not succeed.

- ◆ *Have a unique offer.* If you can offer something of value that no one else is offering, you are more likely to be successful. If you are cold calling with the same offer as everyone else, you will be facing an uphill battle from the start. The worst call someone can make is to a home offering 5.9 percent on a home equity line ten minutes after the home received the same phone call from another solicitor.

◆ *Qualify quickly.* Have a brief statement ready to frame the offer and/or qualify the prospect. Do not waste your time probing non-qualified prospects and putting them in the position to say no further down the line when it is more uncomfortable. Find out quickly whether they are in a position to purchase your product or service with a statement such as, *"If I presented a way to build a retirement plan more quickly, would this be important to you?"*

◆ *Do not sell by voice or e-mail.* Today you are more and more likely to reach a voice mail (or send an e-mail) when making the initial call. If you state your case over the phone (or computer) before you reach your target live, you are much less likely to receive a return phone call or e-mail. Give them a reason to return your call instead of an excuse not to return the call. Your message may be as simple as leaving a name and phone number or a short statement such as, *"I have a compelling offer for you/your firm."*

◆ *Accomplish the research step before making the call.* Just because you don't know your target personally doesn't mean that you cannot find out something about them. For example, if you are calling a law firm, you might start with: *"I noticed on your website that you are the leading employment law firm in this area."* In the Internet age it is easier and easier to find information on our targets.

◆ *Attempt to warm up the cold call.* Before attempting to meet with a new client, try several points of contact via faxes, emails, letters and/or flyers that are designed to familiarize the target with your company and/or your product. It is much more difficult to garner their attention if they have never heard of you or your company when you are attempting to make the first live contact.

◆ *Know what you are going to say.* If you sound hesitant over the phone or in person, you will not move to stage two. Successful businesses react to those who have confidence. You cannot project confidence if you don't know what you are going to say— especially with regard to answering their stated objections. This does not mean that you should be reading from a script. Though scripts are helpful in guiding us, a rigid statement is not always appropriate and can hamper us within the needs assessment process. Try recording yourself and listing to your pitch afterwards. This may give you a different perspective and help move you to improve within certain areas of the prospecting process.

♦ *Get to know the person.* Successful sales are derived through the art of developing relationships. Start the process from day one by listening and finding out about their wants, needs and even their interests as an individual. Going back to the lawyer example, if you know they graduated from Georgetown, perhaps you should know something about their basketball team if they played the day before the call. Use positive verbal "body language" to get them talking. For example, if you ask a question you must invoke a pause to give them the time to respond.

Above all, you must take these final two steps to be successful in cold calling. If you do not achieve some level of success, your call reluctance fears will be confirmed and you will not be motivated to move beyond these fears in the long run. The keys to final success? Asking (at the right moment) and following up. If you don't ask, you will never sell and if you do not follow-up, you will waste the progress made during the prospecting stage. Our time is way too precious to not take advantage of what we have accomplished yesterday and the day before.

Networking skills for success

Networking—Those who are great at it make more money, plain and simple. In this section, we will actually turn to a nationally known expert to help impart the basic skills necessary to improve your networking effectiveness. Lynne Waymon a national speaker and expert on networking skills, offers these basic tips:

#1 No-No

Don't say, "I'm too busy," or "I'm too broke," or "I'm too bashful."

#1 Know-How

Join at least two professional associations. One will be a "peer group" so you can learn and grow with others in your industry. The other will be an association that serves your target market. Plan strategically how you can best leverage your membership in both organizations by choosing involvement that gives you visibility and showcases your character and competence.

#2 No-No

Don't answer the often asked, "What do you do?" with a job category, job title, job jargon, or the name of your company.

2 Know-How

Make your answers (you'll probably have several) short, snappy, memorable, jargon-free, interesting, and crystal clear. Give a talent (one of your many) and then in the second sentence show how you solved a problem, saved the day or served the client. As a speaker I might say, "I show lawyers and CPAs how to bring in the business. Last week when I spoke at the annual marketing retreat of a CPA firm in Baltimore my client said, 'I have never seen these folks so animated and involved.'"

#3 No-No

When someone asks, "What's new?" don't ever say, "Not much. Same old thing. Been working really hard . . ."

#3 Know-How

Be prepared—to be spontaneous. You say you weren't born with the gift of gab? Think of topics ahead of time—topics that you're eager to talk about because of who you are and where you've been and what you're looking for. Respond to "What's new?" with ideas, information, recent successes, inquiries about resources you're looking for. In short, prepare an "agenda" so your small talk is smart talk.

#4 No-No

When you've forgotten someone's name, don't ever say, "I'm sorry. I can't remember your name."

#4 Know-How

If you "blank" on a name, you've got three choices. Don't you often remember the topic, even though you can't recall the name? So say, "Great to see you again. How was your trip to New Mexico?" Or say, "I'm Lynne, Lynne Waymon. We sat next to each other last month." Or say with enthusiasm and warmth, "Hi. I remember you. Tell me your name again."

#5 No-No

Don't go for a cardboard connection—kidding yourself that you're "networking" just because you handed out 23 business cards.

#5 Know-How

Pour your energy into making a conversational connection. Look for a reason to hand out your business card. As you listen, ask yourself what resources you have or people you know that you could introduce the other person to. When you listen generously you don't need excuses for asking for a business card and/or to re-connect—you've got real reasons. "I'll send you that article on how to market your website." Or, "Here's my card. Thanks so much for sending me the name of your book agent." Or "I'll e-mail you with Bill's name and address. Glad I could help you find what you needed."

Whether you love it or hate it, were born with the gift of gab or just fake it, networking know-how is crucial to your success in the business world. With a little practice, you can make networking an art, not an accident.

Now we will add a few more points that will further reinforce Lynne's comments.

◆ Be alert and prepare for networking opportunities. Do not walk into situations blindly and expect to "wing-it." Research your target audience and do as much additional legwork ahead of time as possible.

◆ Be confident in your approach. If you approach others hesitantly, they will be less likely to respond with enthusiasm.

◆ Do not interrupt or monopolize their time when it is not warranted. Be aware of the person's body language for signs their mind is somewhere else (such as looking at their watch while you are speaking).

> *"The single characteristic shared by all successful people*
> *I've met is the ability to create and nurture a network,"*
> Harvey Mackay

(Lynne Waymon is a professional speaker and author who specializes in business positioning and growth through Strategic Networking—www.ContactsCount.com; 1-800-352-2939.)

First impressions

You only have one chance to make a first impression. All the greatest marketing and networking tools in the world will not work if you cannot get to first base with a prospect. This is true whether your first impression is made face-to-face, on the phone or via an e-mail. The guidelines are simple, but they are also very important.

- ◆ *Voice mail.* A topic covered in more detail within other sections of this book, many first impressions are garnered through either your voice mail message or leaving a message on the voice mail of your prospect. Is your message compelling? Is it unique? Do you sound enthusiastic, yet professional? Is it appropriate for your target audience?

- ◆ *Email.* Make sure your first e-mail to a prospect is professionally worded (and spellchecked), not too verbose and not laden with promises that cannot be delivered. You must strike a balance between garnering response (making a compelling offer) and sending a message that is seen as too grandiose or a cheap marketing gimmick.

- ◆ *On the phone.* Be polite and non-obtrusive, especially if you do not have a phone appointment. Ask if this is a good time to talk and offer to reschedule if it is not. Make your voice "up-beat" but not so that it seems not believable. Above all, ask questions and try to engage the prospect to talk about what is important to them. There is nothing that turns a prospect off faster than someone "spilling out" a sales pitch before they have even found out if the prospect is interested or qualifies.

- ◆ *In person.* Face-to-face interaction brings other aspects of making a first impression into play—including dress, body language and even your handshake. It is important to mirror the prospect as much as possible—though in the case of dress it is probably better to be dressed slightly "above" the prospect than "below." In these days of business casual offices, it is not unreasonable to call ahead to uncover the dress code of the office and how the prospect prefers you to dress. If the prospect strikes a formal pose—leaning forward with their hands clasped—it is not a good idea to sit back in your chair with your hands behind your head. Likewise, if the prospect keeps the meeting formal and acts as though there is little time, start with a statement as to the fact that you recognize how valuable their time is and that you will take as little time as possible. Continue to stick to business as much as possible in this case.

Listening skills—the key to sales

For those of us who would like to see our sales levels continue to increase every month, the secret lies within ancient Greek philosophy:

We were given two ears and one mouth
so that we can listen twice as much as we talk.

Anyone who has attended Xerox's original sales course will tell you that the *Art of Sales* is really the *Art of Listening*. There is also no doubt about the fact that the reason most salespeople are reluctant to ask for the business is they have not fully comprehended a consumer's needs to the point that they are confident that they can fulfill those needs. When we understand our target's needs, we are in a position to give our target something of value that will invoke what is termed the *law of reciprocity*. When we have invoked this law, asking becomes so much more comfortable.

Within sales we spend so much time planning actions and taking actions, yet we do very little thinking about listening. After all, we have two ears, why would we need to practice such a simple task?

If it is so simple, then why do we perform this job so poorly? The answer is that most people spend the majority of their time thinking about their own needs and how to fill those needs. When a salesperson is listening to a client, the salesperson is thinking:

"I wish they would finish so that I can get on with this process."

When we fill our mind with these thoughts, we are not listening and are missing the opportunities to achieve the goals that are clouding our minds and hampering our listening skills. It is a vicious cycle: the less we listen, the less we succeed and the more we worry about success and the less we listen.

How can we break out of this vicious cycle? Simple! We need to follow a few rules that will help us concentrate on listening and more importantly let our clients know that we care about their needs.

- ◆ *Get ready to listen in a place that is conducive to listening.* Many times the environment for listening is so distracting it makes it impossible to concentrate on the task at hand. If we are using the phone as a communication device, make sure we are in a room that is quiet and an urgent project is not staring us in the face as we are talking. For face-to-face conversations, it may be necessary to move from our desk to a neutral environment such as a conference room. Certainly, a person's home with kids running around and the television blasting does not represent an ideal listening environment.

◆ *Use affirmative body language to show your target that you are interested.* Affirmative body language includes leaning forward in your chair and nodding affirmatively when your target arrives at key points in their presentation.

◆ *Ask questions that demonstrate your commitment to listen to their feedback.* These questions might include asking them for their opinion on a particular topic. We demonstrate our commitment to listening by more than just asking for their opinion, but by indicating how important their opinion is to us: *I really value your feedback*; or *Your feedback is very important in helping me select the correct course of action.*

◆ *Take notes while the person is speaking.* Taking notes will help your retention as well as letting your target know that you are interested in retaining the information for future reference. Get used to carrying a pad with you at all times.

◆ *Repeat important points.* If the question provides an important response, do not hesitate to repeat this information for emphasis and comprehension. For example, if the prospect says that speed is the most important aspect of service, you might state: *You have indicated that speed is important to you.* This may lead to other questions or clarifications, such as: *What do you consider fast service?* or *Can you give me an example of a time that lack of a rapid response caused disruptions in your business?*

◆ *Give them time.* If they are answering a question, give them the time to finish—even if they get off-track. You lose credibility by cutting them short when you asked the question in the first place. Instead of saying, *That is not what I meant . . .* try *That is important information and I am also interested in hearing about . . .*

◆ *Thank them for their feedback.* At regular intervals, thank your target for letting you know what is important to them. Being gracious is important so that your clients know you appreciate their participation in the process. Do not take for granted their help. Many clients are not interested in making your task easier—they want you to earn your paycheck by doing such things as reading their minds. If you make the wrong decision based upon incomplete information, this puts you at fault in their eyes.

A positive, supportive relationship will facilitate two way communication. The *Art of Sales* is the *Art of Listening*, and listening is more than an art—it can be considered a skill we all must learn to master in order to succeed. It is a skill most of us ignore with dire consequences. Without this skill, we cannot deliver value and value delivery is key to achieving maximum synergy.

Needs assessment—why you need to listen

You will note in our treatment of sales skills we spend little time investigating closing techniques. Many sales training courses focus on closing skills and have institutionalized closing techniques—from the alternative close (*Do you want to meet Monday or Friday?*) or the urgency close (*We only have one left!*). We do not feel that closing techniques are essential to the sales process. Yes, we must ask for the business. The most important reason that we do not ask is that we have not given the target enough value. And we cannot give this value because we have not found their real needs.

True synergy requires that we deliver value. We cannot deliver value unless we match our product or service to the needs of our clients. How do we discover these needs? By listening and developing a relationship. We listen and develop a relationship by asking questions. What kind of questions might we ask?

◆ Questions that enable us to determine if this is the right time to proceed. We call these enabling questions. They are quite simple such as: *Is this a good time for me to ask you a few questions so that I can better help you achieve your goals?*

◆ Questions that enable us to determine the needs of the prospect. These questions might probe in several areas, such as:
  • What is their time frame?
  • What shopping have they done already?
  • What aspect of the product or service is most important to them?
  • Do they have any previous experiences?
  • If they could change anything about their present situation, what would it be?

◆ Questions that help us develop a relationship. These questions help us develop a human aspect to our clients. For example, if they are looking for a home equity loan:
  • What are they trying to accomplish?
  • What are they going to do with the money?

- • If they are going to purchase a car, what kind?
- • What kind of car do they have now?
- • Have you owned the same model?
- • You can see how the line of questioning might work if they were funding their child's college tuition.

◆ Questions that help us determine when and why they are going to take action.

- • Have you made a decision to proceed?
- • When do you expect to make a decision?
- • What information do you need in order to make a decision?

◆ Questions that do not threaten the prospect. If the question is of a sensitive nature, explain the importance of the information before you ask the question. Give them a chance not to answer or to prepare emotionally for a response. They are more likely to answer tough questions if they know there is a logical reason to provide the information, especially one that will help them succeed in the long run.

Whether we are facing an objection or just trying to obtain an appointment, our questioning skills will be imperative to our success in the overall needs assessment process. If you do not have a list of 50 or 100 questions you ask prospects on a regular basis, you are most likely not probing deeply enough. The questions must come naturally—they should not be scripted. No one has developed a relationship reading a script.

Telephone skills—a sales skill unlocks the door to marketing

Do you want to talk about stress? Nothing is more stressful than receiving a stone cold phone inquiry and knowing that you have precious few seconds to develop rapport and set an appointment. The telephone is definitely the most difficult of all marketing tools to master. When you meet a prospect over lunch, you have time to establish a working and/or personal relationship. In person you can read someone's body language and social style.

Over the phone, you must be able to read someone's intentions through long-distance telepathy. You must then be prepared to react to need statements and deliver value within seconds. Talk about pressure!

On the other hand, there is no doubt that the telephone can be an extremely effective marketing tool if used correctly. The telephone is a useful tool for general prospecting, obtaining face-to-face appointments, effecting customer service/follow-up programs and, in many industries, for effecting a complete start-to-finish sales cycle.

In real life, many business people consider the phone something from which to hide. The phone rings and they freeze. Others can't wait to get on the phone and book an appointment. It is the use of this basic tool that can make the difference between a mediocre producer and a superstar. In this section, we will present some very basic telephone techniques that one must follow in order to successfully implement any marketing and/or sales program via the telephone.

- ◆ *Be up all the time*. The secret to successful telephone sales is to be *up* all the time. Many feel that their prices or experience are what will attract someone over the phone. Yet, consumer surveys continuously show that people are sold over the phone by an empathetic voice. In other words, they buy from those they like. Being *up* is not always easy. We know what your offices are like. Sometimes there is someone screaming in the hall or someone else jumping out the window. Still, you must pick up the phone and let the person on the other line know how glad you are to receive their call. And it is not what you say. Plenty of people answer the phone and say that *it is a great day*. If you are feeling low and say it is a great day, more often than not, that sounds worse than yelling at the caller. Reading from scripts can be counterproductive with regard to showing human emotions necessary to enthrall your prospects. The long-term solution? Don't answer the phone until you are ready—emotionally and substantively.

- ◆ *Do not antagonize the antagonizer*. Yes, you will deal with difficult responses over the phone. They may range from do not call me again in reaction to a cold call, to a raging complaint at the time you are calling for a referral. Do not argue or raise your voice to match the emotions of the caller. Your task is to show empathy and remain calm in such a way that will enable you to calm down the prospect so that you can help fill their needs. Remain positive and refrain from negative statements such as *"That was not my job."*

- ◆ *Ask their permission before taking an action*. Do not put the caller on hold or transfer the call without asking their permission to take such an action—even if it is obvious. And if you do transfer someone, remain on the line to make sure the two parties connect before you disengage from the conversation. Nothing is worse than a caller being transferred to the wrong place.

- ◆ *Keep the sound effects down*. Many do not realize what it sounds like to the caller when you clear your throat, chew gum or make other "subconscious" noises. The caller may be just jumping at the chance to end the conversation because of a simple reason such as this. This possibility presents an argument for recording phone conversations and listening later on so that you can detect flaws within your phone mannerisms and presentations.

◆ *Be ready for a gatekeeper.* A gatekeeper may actually determine whether you will ever be able to use the phone as a marketing and/or sales tool. During the business day it may be impossible to reach someone's voice mail directly without going through a gatekeeper. This means that you must be able to sell someone else before moving to the prospect. Sometimes we have a tendency to be short or rude because this person does not occupy the same status as our prospect. *Big mistake.* Develop a relationship with the gatekeeper and be ready to demonstrate why it is important their "protectee" should speak with you personally. A gatekeeper on your side is a resource at your disposal—as opposed to a second obstacle.

◆ *Follow-up.* The secret to great sales—Intelligence . . . Great looks . . . None of the above! Just follow-up with vengeance. Following up is a basic business principle, and it definitely seems to be a lost art in America. It is done so poorly in this day and age, any attempt to shine in this regard will actually exceed your customer's expectations.

◆ *Control the conversation by listening.* The art of sales is rightly known as the art of listening. The person in control of the conversation is not talking. The person in control is learning something. You may not know this but anytime you are talking too much over the phone, the caller on the other line has turned you off mentally. If they had a remote control they would just switch stations.

◆ *Ask questions.* You get someone else to talk by asking questions. This means that you must have your questions prepared in advance and committed to memory. Asking questions is more than a sales technique, it is a way of life. There are some people who are so adept at answering questions with other questions, people swear that they have never given a straight answer in their life. If they were asked for their last wish in the electric chair, they would say: *Why do you ask?*

◆ *Use enabling statements.* Just don't start asking questions. This will be considered rude by the caller, whose main purpose is to learn something from you. You must *ask for the right to ask* which entails the use of an enabling statement. A simple enabling statement would ask if it is all right to ask a few questions so that you are able to provide them with the correct information.

◆ *Have a quick, concise summary of your benefit statement.* For those who are not inclined to listen for more than a few seconds, you must be ready with an important statement/question that will enable you to draw the prospect into the conversation. Such a statement might be—*"Could you use a few more customers in the next month?"* or *"Do you find that you cannot get enough done by the end of each day?"* Ask yourself, what will the customer gain if they listen to my call?

◆ *Don't forget to close.* All the questions in the world are not worth anything unless you recognize the opportunities to close. The purpose of questions is to uncover needs. Closing is not a matter of rote techniques such as the alternative close (today or tomorrow) or the Ben Franklin close (lets weigh the benefits). It is a matter of filling a need at the proper time. And, after you get the appointment or move to the next stage, do not continue to close. Too many people have lost sales because they kept talking after the sales task was complete. Too many people have also lost sales because they tried to educate over the phone and missed their chance to obtain the appointment. If you turn over all your value, why would they not use this information to get a better deal somewhere else?

◆ *Practice, Practice, Practice.* Yes, telephone sales is pressure. You must meet an objective with very little to go on and with very little time. But you do have an advantage. You know what the person on the other end of the line is going to say—*What's the cost?* If you know what they are going to say, it is a simple matter to devise a reply that will stop and make them think. *Do you want the cost in quantum components or Klingon '32s? Have you fully studied the impact of this cost upon your financial situation? What price are you looking for? What price quotes have you already received?* When you find something that works for you, make sure you make it part of your long-term presentation and share your success with others within your office.

◆ *Don't forget to say thank you.* Throughout the conversation you should be asking permission (please) for their time and thanking them for the use of this time and for their substantive input. You are using your prospect's most precious resources—time and knowledge. Do not end a conversation without recognizing this fact.

Have you ever hung up the phone and then said to yourself, *I should have said that!* There is a basic rule of telephone sales: You can't get the conversation back. You must practice, practice and practice some more. Role playing with your peers is an excellent way of furthering your telephone skills. The alternative? Less sales and more stress!

Scripts—another sales tool for success

As we will indicate within the coaching section, it is sometimes very difficult to discover why a salesperson is not succeeding. Though discovering the root of the problem can represent quite a dilemma, we do have one major advantage in sales. We know what the customer or target is likely to say. When we receive a phone call from a prospect, the customer will say the following phrase in some form or fashion more than 90 percent of the time:

What is your price for _____?

Common objections include: price, programs, prejudice, previous bad experience, loyalty and the target not being qualified. Because the responses are so predictable, it becomes easy to design common responses that will help the salesperson fashion statements that will be right on target.

The most rigid of these responses are called scripts. Scripting is most often used in telemarketing. When you get a call at dinner hour, the person on the other side of the phone is likely to be reading from a script. This is why they seem to be lost when they reach Jerry Seinfeld on the other side of the line and Jerry is asking for their home phone number so that he can call them back later!

Properly used, scripts can be very effective instruments for those who have not fully developed long-term relationship skills. They certainly will help anyone over the phone because we all forget certain important questions now and then, such as: *What is your name and phone number?* Of course, they must be used properly. We don't want our salespeople to say to the customer: *Hold on while I get my script.* Scripts are most effective when not repeated verbatim. They are to be used as guidelines to help design a response to fit a particular situation. Even though we do know what the target is going to say, generally each situation will be different in presentation and response.

Scripts make excellent vehicles to give rise to role-playing situations during sales meetings. We can test how certain responses seem to flow well and others do not fit. Certainly a script is more effective than simply letting the salesperson listen to you say it on the street or asking about situations after they happen and telling them what they should have said. Let's give them a comprehensive basis for response—up front.

Scripts represent only one tool that you might find helpful in helping solve the age-old question: *Why no production?* As in any other solution, not having the correct tools at your disposal can be a significant problem, especially when we are trying to increase our levels of production. When production levels drop or someone is not performing, we tend to scramble for solutions. If we expect our salespeople to be prepared, shouldn't we do the same? We can be prepared by giving them the tools necessary to succeed when faced with overcoming objections, call reluctance and the other obstacles of the sales process.

Question all you want, you still have to ask

Major companies and associations hire trainers to present courses to their sales personnel. During these sessions, they hold discussions regarding objections, closing statements, telephone sales or marketing techniques. The truth is, the trainers would be a lot more effective if they could stand in front of these sales-people with a hammer and hit them on the head while screaming—

ASK FOR THE BUSINESS!!!

Every salesperson would increase their sales 20 percent or more if they would just ask more often. Every manager would increase their recruiting efforts 20 percent or more if they would just ask more often. Every sales manager and every salesperson knows this. So why don't they ask more often?

Most would say that the majority of sales personnel do not ask for the business because they are afraid of rejection. They do not want to hear the word *no* and be seen as a failure. The truth is that our salespeople are not afraid of failure. They are afraid of success. We know this because if they do not ask they are assured of failure. How can you get any business when you don't ask? If they ask, they may actually get involved in all the headaches!

Those who are used to high levels of success cannot understand why someone would dress for success, learn everything they need to know and then run around all day and talk to hundreds of people without asking for business. Yet, this happens everyday.

One reason why these people are hesitant to ask is that they feel unworthy. They feel unworthy because they have not delivered enough value to their targets (synergy rule number seven). It is very uncomfortable to say, *"Can I have the sale?"* when you have not delivered any more than the last person who visited. It is certainly very uncomfortable to say this when the person has a long-term relationship with someone else who has delivered much value over the years. Those who deliver value invoke the *law of reciprocity.*

Let's take a look at this simple statement in response to a phone inquiry:

"I work on referrals. Do you know anyone
else who is looking to purchase?"

Simple statement, but uncomfortable and ineffective. Now let us first deliver value.

"Did you read the article I faxed on repairing credit
in preparation for buying? Did you find it valuable
with regard to your financial situation?"

"Yes. It was great. I never had anyone explain what
I can do to help us in our situation. Before reading
this, we felt alone in our problem. Now we realize
that there are many others with our predicament."

"Do you know anyone else who could use this type
of information? As you know I specialize in helping people
like yourselves who are going through this process."

The first example asks for help when there is no positive standing. It is a "ME" statement all the way—*I work on referrals.* The second statement is a natural transition from the delivery of value—*Is there anyone else we can help here?*

If you are completely lost as to why you are not asking more often, we might suggest that you first determine whether you are delivering enough value. The delivery of flyers or advertisements is not a value mechanism. Generating leads for your business clients is a perfect example of value. So are seminars, articles, newsletters and other sources of information.

Newsletters provide an opportunity for a business to provide value for their clients—if they deliver tips designed to increase productivity and not just recipes and handy household hints. The ultimate value is to show someone else how to increase their business or simplify their lives (especially if your target is businesses or salespeople). It is easier to ask for the business when you are delivering valuable financial advice—whether you are working with the direct public and asking for their business or referrals or you are working with long-term business clients such as financial planners or large relocation companies. When you deliver significant value you will never be uncomfortable again.

Not sure what value you can deliver that will make you seem different from your competition. The key is being unique or different. How are you different as a company? As an individual? What are your particular areas of expertise? Dig deep—are you a computer or public speaking expert? Are you a retired golf pro? Use your strengths in such a way that you can differentiate yourself from your competitors.

Let us also explore how we can ask so that we are more likely to achieve results. In other words—

All asking is not the same!

Make sure the time is right. At this juncture we will assume that you have delivered value and have developed the right to ask. Remember, just because you have delivered value does not mean that you are going to achieve a positive response.

Timing is almost everything in sales. If the elevator door is just about to close and you say, *"Can I have some business or a referral?"* you are not going to have much success. Make sure that you set aside time in order to explore the topic with the client. Do not add the topic to the agenda with a hundred others.

Let them know how important the topic is to you. Asking for business in passing does not indicate to the client that their business or a referral is important to you. Just stating, *"I'd like to do business with you,"* is not going to elicit a strong enough response.

Before you ask, let the client know how important they are. Thank them for the business they have referred. Tell them that doing business with them is a major goal of your business plan. You must not merely set aside the time, you must let them know why this time is so significant.

Be specific. Many times we lose out on more business because we assume the client knows everything we are thinking and desire. They don't. It is not unusual for us to say, *"I would like business from you."* This is not enough.

We must state what specific actions we want. Of course, to do this we must know what specific actions we desire. Do we want the client to make phone calls on our behalf? Do we want to accomplish a joint mailing? Do we want their next transaction?

Have a goal and clue our client in. Knowing what particular action we would like our client to take assumes that we have a particular goal. If your goal is 50 percent of your business from personal referrals, let your client know. The best clients can become advocates by letting them be a part of your dreams. Now they are part of your team—rather than merely a satisfied customer.

Make sure they are 100 percent satisfied. Don't assume they are satisfied and then ask. Ask if everything is going (or went) the way they desired. Ask if there is anything else you can do to serve them. Ask if there is anything you should have done differently. Asking for a referral when there is a question lingering in their mind sets up an exercise in futility.

Thank them, thank them and thank them! Let them know how important the last referral was, but in a unique way. Thank you notes and/or flowers are certainly a good practice but unique gifts are really special in this regard. Find out your customer's favorite restaurant and send a gift certificate. What about a special gift from their favorite travel destination? Put some thought into the present rather than churning out mass produced *thank yous*.

If you are asking for the business on a consistent basis, you are ahead of 80 percent of the sales population. If you take care of all of these asking considerations you will be in the top one percent of all producers. The key to achieving ultimate production levels is asking everyone on a consistent basis and doing it in the right way at the right time and with the right reward.

If you merely add a few of these practices to your repertoire you will be way ahead of the competition. Remember, if you don't ask in the right way, someone else will!

When you ask you will encounter objections

In many respects, selling can be seen as a series of obstacles. You must find a potential customer, convince them that this is the right time to purchase and mold the right offer. It may seem as though you must start from square one after each obstacle is surmounted. Your skills with regard to handling each challenge may well determine your long-term success in sales. Many of these skills will fall within the realm of overcoming objections. If there were no objections, then there would be no sale in process.

Objections are good. Dealing with objections may seem to be a trying exercise, yet these actions actually symbolize progress within the sales process. Those who are not selling or asking for the business will be the recipient of no objections. Those who are selling will be the recipient of many. No matter what the response, the point is that the person asked for the business and the objection was a direct result of a positive action. If the question was never asked, then the objection would never have been voiced.

Not all objections can be answered. Good salespeople recognize when to let go. Not overcoming an objection is a sign of effectiveness, not a sign of weakness. Many waste their most significant resource—time—and ruin relationships by pressing the issue when there is little or no hope of a solution. It is wrong to continue to press the issue when there is little hope of coming out on top. The time you invest with little chance of reward could be better spent marketing sources that have better potential for you.

Here is an example of an objection that cannot be answered—

"My wife is a stockbroker and handles our portfolio."

End of story, move on. Unless you think the target's wife may make a good synergy marketing partner (those synergy marketing rules, again!) there may be no value in continuing to forge a long-term relationship.

We should note that moving on from a prospect because you could not answer an objection does not mean that you cannot receive something of value from that prospect. For example, perhaps they do not need to list on your Internet site because they already have enough business. Ask them for a referral to a company that might need more business.

Never disagree. People's perceptions are just that, perceptions. They are neither right nor wrong. The first time you put yourself in the position of challenging their perception you will lose credibility. Never say—*Price isn't important, my value is important.* Do say that you understand why they feel price is important.

You must listen. You must first seek to understand the importance of the objection and to do this you must listen and understand. After all, isn't listening the key to sales? No one can sell without listening. Within the sales process there is no more important juncture for which listening is necessary than for the identification of objections. Basically, when a target is stating their objection they are giving you a pathway to success. It is here that you must first be sure to understand their response before trying to fashion a plan of action. The key to listening is to ask questions. Listening should be followed with questions as to why this objection is important to them, such as:

What has this company done to earn your loyalty?

You must empathize with their position. Now that you understand the basis for their conclusion, be empathetic. Say things such as, *"I understand how your present relationship is important to you."* Their answer will give you a better foundation for answering the objection and uncovering other significant factors.

Fill their needs. Recognize that a statement of objection is a statement of need. If they say that they are happy with their present relationship, find out what needs this relationship fills and what needs are unfulfilled.

In what ways could your present company improve their service?

Know the objections you will encounter. We have an advantage when trying to overcome objections because we should always be aware of the realm of possibilities. Objections are good because they are a necessary step within the sales process and because there are a limited number of objections for which to prepare. Here are some general categories of objections:

◆ price—the product costs too much;
◆ product—I don't like whole life insurance;
◆ loyalty—I only purchase Fords;
◆ prejudice—I don't like working with small companies;
◆ unfamiliarity—I have never heard of your company;
◆ need—I don't need any more business right now; and,
◆ timing—I want to think about it for awhile.

Almost all objections will exist within these basic categories. Because we know what is coming it makes it easier to be prepared with a response—after our questioning process has isolated the real needs.

Practice, practice, practice. Nothing will halt the sales process faster than a fumbling objection response:

I didn't realize that anyone could have too
much business in this tough environment.

Caught by surprise? Shouldn't you know about how well your target is doing? It doesn't matter if this is the first time you met the potential buyer or that person is your relative, you should be prepared for an objection.

A quick and decisive response to the objection makes all the difference in the world when leading the sales process. When we say that some salespeople can sell anything to anybody, we really mean that they are ready for any objection. Practicing objection responses helps us develop the right tone and timing. Above all, the salesperson must exhibit an air of confidence in their response. They must sound as if they really believe what they are saying. The response must be quick and deliberate in order to evoke this impression. Confidence and timing come with practice.

◆ Know what to say when someone is concerned with the price;

◆ Know what to say when someone is loyal to another person or company.

Use facts. It is important to appear as an expert when you present objection responses (without discrediting the target). For example, if you are in Internet sales, know how quickly Internet use is growing and what actions their competitors are taking with regard to on-line marketing. If they are unfamiliar with your company, where do you rank nationally/locally? Present facts as to the strength of your company's financial position.

When the time comes, negotiate. Sometimes the process of sales can be a series of negotiations. As you answer their objections, you will will move into the negotiation stage. This is why it is important to understand their objections and their needs. You will rarely be successful negotiating unless you know what the other side desires. Anytime you find out what they want before you make an offer, you have the upper hand. Of course, the real goal of successful negotiations is for both sides to achieve their objectives. If both sides cannot win at the same time, there may be no basis for a long-term relationship.

Remember, how well you handle the objection process is a good indication of how well you will be in position to close the sale. If objections stop you from selling but are not stopping your peers, is their approach different? Don't blame your lack of success on the market, your product, your price or your customers. You can't change any of these things. You can change how you react to your customers' objections.

Selling price or value

As we move into the age of technology, we are certainly going to witness a whole new wave of competition. From affinity relationships to one-stop shopping conglomerates to the Internet, there is no doubt that all potential customers are going to have a greater choice in selecting services and products. Some of these will be efficient mechanisms for price comparisons. At some point in your planning process, you will have to make this decision—

Are you going to be a low cost or a full-service value provider?

If you are going to sell your services at the lowest price, get on the *Internet* and advertise your fees to the world. If you are going to be a full-service provider, you will have to learn how to *sell without price.* How do you do that? Here are a few suggestions:

Let your sales efforts set the tone. Complaining about your customers being so price conscious? Examine your advertising. Is it designed to compete based upon price? Are you attracting customers who are going to be interested solely in your price? Yes, there is a certain class of customers who are extremely price sensitive. Why would you spend your time and money attracting them if you would like to be a full-service value provider?

Deal with people you know. Do you spend tons of money and time advertising to the world and making the phone ring with people you don't know? Are you making cold calls over the phone? While you do this are you ignoring previous customers because you don't have time? Deal with the people within your sphere of influence. People you don't know will be focused upon price because there is no basis for a relationship. Focusing upon your *sphere of influence* ensures that you won't waste the time you have spent building relationships in the past.

Have the right attitude. Do you have the feeling that you are price shopped harder than anyone else? Forget the woe is me attitude! Every industry has price shoppers—from the airlines to insurance. For which item did you price shop recently? Perhaps a car? The point is that you will turn off more customers because of your attitude about their price shopping than you will with your prices. People do business with people they like. A bad attitude is not likable—period!

If you get called . . . have the skills to find needs. People will always ask about price, mainly because they do not know what else to ask. When they call, have the questions ready to uncover their real needs. Is it education? Is it speed? Is it convenience? Sales is the science of listening. You can't find someone's needs unless you get them to talk. You can't get them to talk unless you ask questions. Have the questions ready and deliver them in a way that is non-threatening and helpful. In other words, be empathetic to their situation so they will like you! And you don't have to reinvent the wheel—if you don't know the questions to ask, others do.

Sell value, value, value. If you are not going to compete based upon price, you better be selling value. *Faster, cheaper and easier* are what everyone sells. What can you add to the equation? Here is a test: Did your last advertising piece offer a discount for your services or something extra for your services? What can you offer—information, additional services or anything to better help meet the customers' need? The great part of additional value is the fact that you do not necessarily have to provide the value. It can be provided by a *synergy partner* (rule number two).

Communicate the value. Sometimes a price issue is raised because the customer does not really understand the value of the product (or the real price, for that matter). We will cover the importance of communication skills during the Management Chapter—however, it is apparent that clear communication is a sales, marketing, customer service and management skill. In this instance, a lack of clear communication can halt the sales process or at least turn it into a price negotiation. When you negotiate to cut your price, you put yourself in a position to deliver less value in the long run.

Value or price. In the long run, every business will have to make the decision regarding whether to focus upon the final maximum synergy rule. Our advice is not to get stuck in between.

Move to the close quickly within the process

Closing represents more than effecting a statement that causes your target to take action. If it were that simple, sales training courses that focus upon teaching closing techniques such as the "forced-choice" close (assuming the sale is done and asking them to choose product specifications) would be effective. They are not. Closing is part of a longer-term process that starts with determining your target, assessing their needs (see needs assessment and listening) and asking for the business at the point we deliver the right amount of value (see asking for the business and value).

We must move this analysis one step further. Salespeople sell more when they close consistently. But great salespeople get in front of more people and that is another reason why they sell more. You must be in front of the target audience before you can learn their needs, deliver value and then ask.

This is exactly the reason why some seem to sell more consistently year after year. These sales superstars move into a new job, a new territory or sell a new product more quickly and more effectively than anyone else. Others take their time to study, learn and plan while the top producers forge ahead and make more money. These top producers actually shorten the sales process. What does this mean?

For one, top producers make calls more quickly within the sales process. They lack most aspects of call reluctance. Those with a healthy dose of call reluctance tend to make sure they:

◆ fully understand their product;
◆ hone their pitches;

◆ perfect their marketing materials; and,

◆ locate the perfect target(s) to call upon.

This is not to say that top producers move before they understand their product or use poor marketing materials or methods. It just means that everything does not have to be perfect before they act. A sales manager can always determine those with call reluctance. They make statements such as, *"I can't call, my business cards are not ready."*

Top producers call everyone who may help them. Those with call reluctance may not call upon those in the best position to help them make a sale. For example, those with call reluctance may not call their family because they do not want to give the appearance to their close relatives that they are not doing well. Top producers realize that their closest contacts have a vested interest in helping them achieve success and are not shy about exploiting any resource.

When top producers call, they ask for the appointment more quickly. Those with call reluctance tend to make statements such as:

Would you like me to send you more information?
or
I will call you next week so we can set an appointment.

Top producers forge ahead and just ask for the appointment. If their target is not ready to meet this week or next, they pull their calendar out in any case to make sure they reserve a spot now—rather than later.

Top producers ask for the sale at the appointment. With top salespeople, there is no waiting for follow-up—they always give a chance for their targets to make a decision on the spot. Instead of saying *"Can I call you next week?"* they are more prone to say:

Do you have the information you need to make a decision at this point?
What can I do to help you make a decision on this matter?
What can I do to help you get the process started?

The top producer introduces an element of urgency into the equation. Without appearing too bold or too "pushy," those who earn more tend to interject urgency into the decision-making process in such a way that it appears to benefit the target to move more quickly. It is important that the urgency is not introduced as a benefit to the salesperson.

It would really help me to get this sale on the board this month.

Instead, the top producer will make statements that clarify benefits for the individual such as:

*If we can complete the purchase this week,
we can reduce your tax bill this year.*

*If you can give me the paperwork today, I can get
my office to move more quickly on your behalf.*

These examples clearly demonstrate the dichotomy between someone who is "meandering" through the sales process and someone who is flying through. Top producers actually shorten the sales cycle, while others not only make the cycle longer, they may cause the sale not to happen at all. The longer the process, the more likely a competitor may step in or the target may decide not to act.

Top producers recognize closing or buying signals. The worst mistake we can make when closing is not recognizing when our potential customer is giving us buying signals and continuing to sell past this juncture within the sales process. Recognizing buying signals involves being attentive (for example, paying attention to body language) and invoking responses that test where our prospects are within the process. It is easy to float "trial" language such as, *"Do you have any other questions at this juncture?"* without appearing too aggressive. Many sales have been lost because we were not ready to ask when our prospects were ready to say yes. Believe it or not, we are not required to present our whole sales presentation to be effective.

The message is clear. If you are not making enough money, where could you shorten your sales cycle? Why do you not act when action is possible and more than likely advisable? Do you make excuses such as: *They were not ready* or *I did not have a good enough deal for them.* Every salesperson possesses elements of call reluctance and it is only those who overcome their reluctance who have a chance to move to the status of a top producer. We are talking about more than closing techniques at this juncture—though closing is certainly an integral part of the sales cycle. We are talking about consistently being in a position to close.

The home as a base for marketing and sales

The Internet
Telecommuting
Digital Wireless Communications

What do all of these things have in common? Generally, they were not likely to have a part in your life a short time ago. Ten years from now, what new concepts are likely to dominate our personal and business worlds? It is exciting to guess what may be just around the corner!

We do know that technological advances have put us in a position to accomplish our business differently in the future. How different? If we are to succeed in the future we are in a position that we must integrate many of these advances into our business plans.

Ten years ago those working out of the home were likely to be performing part-time clerical work. Now those working out of their home are just as likely to be running large organizations. Technology has made this possible. When one considers technological progress, working out of one's home will be more likely now more than ever.

So what are the advantages of working out of one's home? Not having to spend several hours in the car certainly is one advantage. With the population growth of the United States continuing, congestion is sure to get worse in the coming years. Those with families are much more likely to be drawn to business situations that allow flexibility with regard to hours and location.

Setting up a home office and succeeding in business with this "set-up" is not as easy as it seems. Many feel they can just close a door and start making phone calls. But to succeed, we will need more than just a home from which to work . . .

You must have the equipment, including:

- ◆ *Phones*. Don't try using one line in a home. You will need a separate business line that can be answered differently and carry a separate message from the home line. You will also need at least one or two extra lines—for a fax machine and modem. Today, a modem line for your phone may very well be integrated into your phone service via a DSL connection—or a high-speed internet connection may be provided through your cable company. A cordless phone will also be very helpful. If you work at home, you will no doubt be wandering around the house at different times. The ability to carry the phone will add flexibility.
- ◆ *A computer*. Not just any computer. If you work out of an office part-time and out of the home part-time, then a laptop may be the answer. This will allow you to carry the computer from station-to-station without having to set-up a more complex networking

situation. Of course, if your main office is integrated into a network a different solution may be needed.

♦ *Fax, printer and scanner.* Think that you might have to purchase another house to fit the equipment? Today, one machine can perform all of these functions, though some combined machines do not have as much *flexibility* as copiers or scanners, especially with regard to handling the duplication of articles and books.

♦ *Filing cabinets and a book case.* You will not save time if you are spending half of your day looking for items that should be organized in files. Make sure you have the equipment necessary to separate and organize business paperwork

♦ A *desk and chair.* Working at the kitchen table just does not work when the ketchup gets spilled. Working at home will also not be effective if you are working at a table while others are eating and having conversations a few inches away.

Putting it together does not mean just throwing the equipment in your recreation room. For instance:

♦ Make sure you have a completely separate work area. Do not think that it is easy to participate in conference calls or meet clients from a kitchen.

♦ Even with today's proliferation of e-mail communication there will be need for vendors such as overnight shipping services. Today's companies are programmed to make regular stops at personal residences.

♦ A home address may not be an advisable part of your advertising scheme. If you do not have a larger, permanent office, consider a P.O. Box for snail mail. 123 Happy Face Lane just may not look good for corporate presentations.

♦ Have an *Web* presence. On the computer anyone can create an atmosphere like a multi-national corporation. Having Internet, e-mail and P.O. Box addresses on materials can make your business look ready to go head-to-head with the big boys.

It is very important for you to be honest with yourself when you set-up your home office environment. Do you have the discipline necessary to wake up and begin working without driving to an office? Can you block out the interruptions that are inevitable, including visits from the neighbors and personal phone calls? Are you able to avoid working within walking distance from your own, personal refrigerator? If you cannot, the time you save commuting can be easily lost and then some. If you do have the discipline—whether you are a part-time salesperson or a seasoned top producer—your home may be the center of your personal and business life in the future.

Time management—you don't get any more

There is no doubt that time is a salesperson's most precious resource. In fact, time is everyone's most precious resource. We never realize how precious time is until we run out of it. George Burns had 100 years, yet he never had time for his final performance.

We all waste too much of our precious resource. Many years ago when I began teaching methods of improving time management skills, I introduced the concept of *1435* in order to prove a major point. What is *1435*? It is the number of minutes left in the day after we waste five minutes. For the average person, we waste over one-third of our workday, either procrastinating or working on tasks that will not help us achieve our long-term objectives.

The key to getting more done? Developing a sense of urgency with regard to what needs to be accomplished. A simple exercise will demonstrate the different state of mind that we must achieve. Imagine your last vacation. The serenity of knowing that you didn't have to check messages or get up at a certain time. Perhaps you had no special agenda. After a few days of unwinding, work was the furthest from your mind (hopefully).

Now think of the day before you left on that vacation. Do you now have a different memory? Was that day a little more stressful? We would venture to say that the day before you left was your most effective time management day of the year. That day you accomplished more than any other. You quickly determined priorities and went about achieving those priorities. If you failed, you would not get out of town on time.

The day before vacation you had an urgency about what needed to get done. The key to better time management is to develop this sense of urgency every day of your life. How do you do that? Perhaps we should take more vacations!

On a more serious note, the first step in getting more done is realizing what you need to accomplish. Once you have a clear mission, you will realize that many of the tasks that now occupy your time are actually keeping you from achieving your goals.

Let's take a look at an example of linking your mission to your actions. Think of a customer you could not move off the fence for weeks or months. Perhaps they purchased. Perhaps they did not. Either way, the process was a waste of your time. Even if there was a sale hanging in the balance, think in terms of the opportunity costs of lost time.

Calculate how many hours you spent on this transaction. The perpetual shopper can consume hundreds of hours of your time. The more time you spend with the customer, the more likely you will feel obligated to keep going to receive a return upon your investment. But what a cost! Hundreds of hours to achieve a paycheck of _____? More significantly, how much could you have earned had you spent these hundreds of hours marketing and working with more productive customers? In reality, the hours that you are spending with shoppers are actually preventing you from marketing and developing relationships that would be much more productive.

So what do you do with the shopper? First, you might accomplish a more thorough job of assessing their goals and needs up front. Perhaps you are encouraging unprofitable relationships by forcing action when the potential customers are not psychologically ready. Simple questions regarding their goals might give you a clue to their intentions. Ask about their last purchasing experience, how long have they thought about purchasing, have they searched before and not purchased and if so, what has changed at this juncture?

One example might be a lawyer that has a client consistently approaching them for "free" legal advice without taking any of the actions necessary for moving ahead with the legal action. Without *blowing them off* or providing poor client service by not returning their phone calls, a few minutes probing whether they have come to a conclusion would be beneficial. If they are not ready, advise them to take certain steps on their own (perhaps they need to see a marriage counselor). If they are ready, move them into an action plan. Do not let them remain in limbo. Nothing creates more stress than wandering aimlessly—for you or for them.

Should you fire these people? Of course not. Nurture the relationship by giving them goals to meet before you become actively involved. If they insist upon monopolizing your time without a reasonable chance of return benefits, refer them to someone else who would appreciate such a referral—perhaps a neophyte. Chances are those who are less experienced have much more time on their hands and can use the experience to learn. What better way to learn customer service and negotiation skills than on live customers (well, almost live). Perhaps you may be entitled to a referral fee if they get lucky.

We've said this over and over, but can't stress it enough, time is our greatest resource. Everyday we waste our time in a variety of ways. If you ask every business person for a self-assessment, almost all of them would reply: I need to manage my time better. We would be remiss in ending this general discussion of time management without adding the following pointers that may help us conserve our most precious resource. If we have more time, we can make more money. What follows are several things you can do to gain more time each day.

Start Dealing With Priorities. Stephen Covey says that our problem is not managing time, it is managing ourselves. We must first decide to deal with matters of importance to us in order to accomplish our mission in life. This means that we may have to stop dealing with urgent matters that may mean more to other actors in our life. Therefore, we must learn to say no when it is appropriate.

Take the time to analyze how much time you spent doing what in a particular week. Write it down. How much time did you spend accomplishing tasks that could be considered essential to your success? The next time you make a list of items to accomplish the next day, prioritize them. Try to accomplish the list in accordance with your own priorities instead of acting on the wishes of others. Start one day at a time and move in the same direction for the whole week.

Identify your goals. Before you can prioritize, you must recognize what is important in your life. Spend some time determining what you would like to accomplish next year and in the long run. Goals should be personal and professional. They must be specific. If you would like to retire: *When? Where? And with how much income?* It is hard to prioritize if you do not determine what is important to you. Most of us move through life without a clear definition of what is important and what is not.

Start the day with a plan. Never leave your house without a plan of action. Each day formulate a checklist of items to accomplish. Sunday is a good time to plan for the week. After you have finished writing, analyze your list. Is it realistic? Can you eliminate items of lesser importance?

At the end of each day, re-analyze your list. Did you accomplish what you had hoped? If not, why not? Are you going to start the next day with the same set of priorities, or did you learn something through today's experience?

Interrupt the interruptions. Many times we cannot work on priorities because we allow others to intervene with their priorities. Sometimes we must learn to say no if the interruption prevents us from accomplishing our objectives. Many feel they are letting others down by putting them off. In reality, if we make them understand the importance of our present task, they will respect our choices. As Stephen Covey says, *First Things First*.

Work on one task at a time. If you are trying to accomplish too many tasks at once, you are likely to get nothing accomplished. Take a good look at your desk or work area. File everything away except for your next priority. Do not stop working on that project until it is finished and filed away. This may mean holding phone calls and putting a halt to the fires you may get called upon to douse. Let someone else keep the office from burning.

Organize—Now! Stop spending your time looking for everything. Organize your office and your life. Put everything in its place and file every day for a few minutes rather than dedicating a whole week to the task at the end of the year. Do not handle papers twice—act on it or trash it.

Every time you put a piece of paper in a file, remove and trash another piece of paper in the same file. Barbara Hemphill, in her famous *Taming the Paper Tiger Series* indicates that the trash can is a major organizational tool. Now the file will not grow bigger than your office. Do not make copies of many memos that are in the memory of the computer. Remember, the goal of a paperless office is why we became automated in the first place.

Hire Someone. If you would like to make a six figure income, then don't spend your time stuffing envelopes and handing out fliers. No matter what it says in the back of magazines, no one ever became rich stuffing envelopes. Hire someone for menial tasks that take your time. Spend your time on the priorities such as marketing and selling.

Don't begin tomorrow with yesterday's task. It is too easy to put off tomorrow what you should have accomplished today. Bad habits are hard to break. Remember, you pared your list to include only priorities. If it was important, get it done. If your list was too ambitious, adjust the list for tomorrow. But tonight, you are working late.

Schedulingit or it won't happen

Every day each one of us takes the same actions we have taken yesterday, last month and last year and miraculously we are expecting a different result. If we interviewed thousands of business people and asked them what is the one area in which they thought they could improve, the vast majority would say they *need to be more organized*. In order to be more organized do you think you will have to take an action tomorrow that will be different from the actions today? Absolutely.

The key to changing your activities is located within a simple tool we all have at our disposal—our calendar. We all have calendars but very few of us use them to make the changes we need made in our lives. To illustrate this point, I would like to encourage you to perform the following exercise. Go over all activities you have scheduled in your calendar for the next 30 days. I predict you will have business appointments, sales meetings, doctors appointments and more.

Now, think of your most important priority. Is it to get more organized? Increase your marketing focus? Further your technical skills? Spend more time with your family? What activities have you scheduled to make this priority happen? If you have not scheduled the time necessary to perform the activities needed to achieve your most important priority, what are the chances that you will be successful in reaching your objective? The answer is obvious.

If developing a comprehensive marketing plan is your top priority, shouldn't the actions necessary for development of this plan occupy at least the same importance within your calendar as your next haircut appointment? My suggestion would be to start blocking time on your schedule so that you will undertake important activities that you do not ordinarily "get to" during a normal business day.

These activities might include the time to learn a new computer software program (or learn how to turn your computer on!), the time to rethink your priorities, the time to develop your network or simply the time to relax. How many of us actually schedule the time we need to relax in this day and age?

Some additional suggestions:

◆ Schedule this activity first thing in the morning. If you schedule it for a later time, it is much more likely to be usurped by your usual crisis of the day. Scheduling it for later in the evening is typically an exercise in futility—as most of us are too tired to accomplish anything of importance this late in the day (such as exercising).

◆ Don't just block out the time, write in the actual activity that you expect to undertake. If you are intending to write a letter, then specify the subject. Just scheduling something broad such as developing a marketing plan is much too general. You might spend most of the time figuring out what to accomplish.

◆ As soon as you finish this activity, schedule the next one immediately. Now that you have written the letter, when are you going to get the letter in the mail? Are you going to follow with a phone call? Think about how many times you moved half-way through an activity and never finished because of an inability to follow-up.

Nothing happens by chance. If you are looking to improve in a particular area, you must undertake the activities necessary to achieve this improvement. What we are looking for here is a commitment to schedule the activities that will move you closer to reaching your goals. Ask yourself, when was the last time that you accomplished something new and important without making a commitment? When was the last time that you finished all the work you had scheduled and then started attacking your long-term priorities?

The answers to these questions are quite obvious. Reworking your schedule will in no way change your life by enabling you to accomplish your dreams. *Schedulingit* is designed to help you move in this direction. Our maximum synergy rules tell us that some tools are more effective than others. Some effective tools we do not use effectively are right under our nose—such as our calendars.

Speed—the must skill for today and tomorrow

We can speculate for days regarding how the future of the business world will affect our lives and our opportunities for success. We know that computers and especially the Internet are going to dominate many industries. With every new business medium there is going to be new challenges and new opportunities.

There is one constant that permeates the progress of modern industry. No matter what advances shape business the basis for this advancement will be *SPEED*. Yes, every move forward seems geared to allow us to react more quickly in the business world.

Through the Internet, one now has access to information that would have taken days, weeks or years to obtain previously. E-mail allows for instantaneous communication and response. So do cell phones, digital paging devices, broadcast faxes and video-conferencing units.

Every year we seem to obtain more timesaving devices but each of these devices seem to rob us of time. For example, cell phones allow us to react to calls from anywhere. They also tie us to a phone on a constant basis. Anyone ever feel that they now can't seem to get away from their work?

Every year seems to resemble a treadmill that goes faster and faster. One thing is certain, the future is not for those who do not react quickly. The consumers of the future will demand instantaneous access to information, quick decisions and instant gratification for their desires. They will demand *SPEED*!

Take a look at the stock market for a confirmation of these trends. The exchanges are looking at trading hours that are basically 20 hours each day. The new stock market leaders are companies that did not even exist a few short years back.

Are you prepared for the speed of the 21st Century? Sometimes it is hard to extrapolate from where one is now standing to the speed of the new century. You may look at yourself and see someone who is prone to procrastination, a technical neophyte and unable to get their hands around the simplest tasks of today let alone the challenges of the future.

Take heart, these characteristics we have described are typical of many business people today. But they will not set well with the advances of the future. You must spend some time now in preparation for success in the speed zone of tomorrow.

Ask yourself: *Can I react quickly to the demands of today's customers?* What advances might change these demands so that you will have to react even more quickly? When you get a call from a prospect, how quickly can you react? A quick reaction in the future will be more than just "returning a phone call," it will be the provision of information and services that instantly bonds you to a customer. It may have been enough to return a phone call ten years ago. With the consumer of tomorrow receiving a barrage of offers of value on a constant basis, the response will have to be right on target in order for the prospect to stop in their tracks and tune out other stimuli.

What if a completely new avenue of competition entered your target market instantaneously? Not just another salesperson, but a Microsoft or the equivalent gorilla. Are you prepared to react quickly and decisively to protect your livelihood? It is certainly hard to protect yourself when there is no telling from which direction the attack will be progressing.

Sound ominous? Absolutely—but remember with every challenge there is an opportunity. The average business person will not be prepared to react to tomorrow's challenges. For those who can react, greater levels of success will be available. This covenant is exactly why 20 percent of the sales force accomplishes 80 percent of the production in almost every industry. The law of evolution assures a high turnover rate for those who cannot meet the demands of the open markets.

It is time for you to decide now what your strategies will be tomorrow. Spend some time studying industry trends and the movements of your competition. Stand ready to move quickly—speed will be essential to succeed in the sales world of tomorrow.

Trends for tomorrow

We are now at the beginning of a new century. Are we in a position to take advantage of the most important trends that will affect businesses in the future? We can think of three tools which might leverage any business person's efforts well beyond the energy expended in order to develop expertise using such a tool. These tools are technology, public speaking and foreign languages. Let's take a closer look at all three.

Technology. There is no doubt that technology is affecting all industries more rapidly as we move to the future. The fastest growing companies are technologies and this means that all industries—from retail to services—are in for some new competition.

If you are going to survive and prosper next year and beyond, you must become part of the technology revolution. This is not to say that we all must do business on the *Internet*. It does mean that we must be utilizing basic technology—including database, e-mail and the graphics necessary to reach our customers effectively.

While many of us are planning to make a major splash using *Internet* technology, many of us do not have an effective way to keep in touch with past and present customers. We spend countless hours converting leads, developing relationships and providing top notch customer service. We then spend more time converting additional cold calls while we ignore contacts with our customer base. Technology gives us the ability to keep in touch with our customer base—effectively and efficiently. In the future, if we don't keep in touch with our customers, someone else will—especially as the trend continues toward larger and larger organizations through merger activity. The larger the company, the more likely they will have a large customer base and a vested interest in retaining that base as well as selling additional products to these customers.

Public Speaking. As much of our competition gets lost in their world of computers, we predict that the art of public speaking will become lost. This is not to say that most of us are proficient or even competent public speakers presently.

In the future, a way to personally connect to our targets will be very significant. Our targets will be bombarded with technological stimuli. Those with a personal touch will have the upper hand.

Why public speaking? Why not telephone calls or one-on-one meetings?

Because a great public speaker stands out from the competition. Anyone can read a script over the phone. A great speaker can move the masses with an impassioned plea. Public speaking is more time effective than other means of selling. Think about selling 100 prospects during a one-hour speech. How long would it take you to get to the same amount of people one at a time? Talk about effective marketing through use of an advanced sales skill.

Foreign Languages. The face of America is changing. The good news is that economic growth will be sustainable because of constant population growth. The bad news is that you may be going after a target that will not exist in large enough numbers ten years down the road.

The number of immigrants reaching our shores has reached a level only seen at the beginning of the century. They are coming from all over the world— from South America to Asia. Soon Spanish speaking Americans will out-number traditional minorities such as Black Americans. Are you ready for such a market influx?

Learning a foreign language (and culture) will enable you to set up partnerships that will keep you busy in the future. This is not to say that the baby boom generation will fall off the face of the earth—but business success is often defined by those who are ahead of market trends. The trend of a new America is clearly around the corner.

There well may be other tools that will help you succeed over the next decades. Yet, it is hard to argue that those who are technologically proficient, can speak a foreign language and can deliver their message effectively in front of a group will not have a major advantage over their competition today and for the foreseeable future.

CHAPTER FIVE
The ABCs of Maximum Synergy
Marketing Tools for Success

"Men do not fail; they stop trying."
Elihu Root

Marketing. There is no more significant setting within the business world in which the application of our maximum synergy rules can be demonstrated to positively impact the increase of our production levels with a corresponding decrease in our levels of stress. In this chapter we will be introducing a variety of marketing tools and demonstrating again and again how maximum synergy can increase your effectiveness. We will begin with a few basic guidelines that apply to all marketing actions.

- *You will do everything else first.* Even though marketing activity is what brings business in the door, most business people (including salespeople) will not make it their highest priority. We tend to get lost in putting out fires and paperwork. We all have enough administrative work to keep us busy forever. However, if business does not come in the door there will be no need to accomplish this work. This sets up what we call the "cycle of sales"—periods in which we have too much business, followed by periods in which we have too little business. This occurs because we market only when we have little else to do and we have no choice. We will term this phenomenon *marketing reluctance.*

- *The world of marketing ideas from which we can choose is infinite.* We could spend days giving ideas to market a particular product. Most of these would represent great business ideas. No one can accomplish all of these. Your job as a salesperson or business owner is to choose the most effective actions and effect these consistently. If you chose too many, consistency will go out the window.

- *You cannot change the world in one day.* If you would like to change the effectiveness of your actions, look for incremental improvements. If there is not enough time in the day to market effectively now, how could you make wholesale changes in any effective manner? Look for the *low-hanging fruit*, or small changes, that can effect marginal amounts of improvement. This is what synergy is all about—making changes that require the least amount of your resources.

◆ *Your marketing activities will not work if you don't believe.* Marketing must be carried out with a positive belief. If you take actions half-heartedly, they will not work and you will be wasting your most precious resources—money and time. Attitude represents the key to implementing any marketing plan. Too many times we give up on a good action because we didn't stick with the plan long enough or never gave it the attention it deserved.

◆ *Marketing and sales are not the same.* Marketing makes the phone ring. Sales represent the actions you take in order to convert the call into a sale. You must take both actions to succeed. Many do not succeed because they do not possess the sales skills to bring produced leads to closure. Yet, they blame the marketing activities for the lack of results. This concept is why we preceded this chapter with one covering the essences of sales. This work would be incomplete without tying marketing and sales together. On the other hand, some marketing activities may produce leads that are harder to close.

◆ *It is not just how many you call.* The purpose of marketing is to get the phone to ring or respond in some other way. The ultimate goal of marketing is to produce revenue. Therefore, the quality of responses is just as important as the quantity of responses. More calls will produce more revenue as long as the right prospects respond at the right time. If more responses are produced from the wrong prospects the overall impact upon earnings is likely to be negative.

◆ *You won't convert marketing leads if you don't ask.* All the marketing leads in the world will not help if you don't ask for the business. The quality of the lead produced does not matter if you do not ask. If you do not ask, you will not succeed.

Advertising synergy

Advertising is a very broad topic that covers many areas that will be dealt with within other sections of this chapter. Though we may think of the broader media (radio, TV) when we consider the subject of advertising, our more specific efforts to market, such as direct mail and faxing, constitute similar forms of advertising that will be governed by the same general guidelines for success. The fact that we are beginning the assessment of marketing rules with this topic is very helpful because it enables us to outline some very broad concepts that will apply again and again as we scrutinize additional subject areas within our analysis of marketing synergy. The concepts are:

Consistency. Advertising must be consistent in three ways. First, there must be numerous points of contact in order for advertising to be effective. This means that one cannot try an advertising method one time and then move on to another target. The points of contact do not have to be the same—we can reach the target through a newspaper advertisement one day and the radio or a fax the next day and the effect can very well be cumulative.

Second, though the points of contact may vary, the message must be consistent throughout. You cannot emphasize added value one day and low prices the next and expect the results of the two contacts to be synergistic.

There must be a consistency of appearance. For example, within print ads, the company or offer must be presented in a consistent way. Large corporations such as IBM or McDonalds spend millions on developing a consistent brand to which the public can identify. If you are an independent business person, your message must be just as consistent (minus the millions, of course).

Simplicity. As proprietors of a business, we are very involved and interested in all facets of our product and its features and benefits. When we present our products to our targets we tend to think they are just as interested. They are not. Our targets are not as interested and do not have the time to wade through the details we would like to present. This is why headlines are so important. Ninety percent or more of what we present will not be read. The solution is to make your advertisements simple and straightforward. If they have to think too much or wade through too much material to arrive at your message or offer, you are going to lose them.

Link features to benefits. Chances are that you know your product well and features are important to you. What is important to your targets is how these features affect them. In other words, your customers think in terms of benefits, not features. For example, you may think it is important to note that your product is lightweight. But what does that mean? It may mean that they will have less visits to the chiropractor when they try to carry it around. It may mean that they can bring something else with them on a trip. This is all part of the needs assessment process.

Call to action (response mechanism). Do not forget synergy rule number six: Do not bother to advertise unless you have a significant call to action. There must be a reason for someone to call you today. Name identification, branding and credibility are important for big companies. Salespeople and small business owners must eat every day and they don't eat unless the phone rings or someone orders on-line. Ask yourself, is your offer compelling? Is it of value to your targets? Is it different (unique) compared to other offers they are receiving? Generally, coupons can be effective tools—but they do not constitute value to anyone except those who are ready to order today. Response mechanisms and value are basic building blocks of synergy.

You don't have to spend all your money. Not all effective advertising is expensive. Through synergy relationships, some advertising is free. What do you have to offer to those who can help you spread the word to your targets? For example, publishing an article may achieve more results than an advertisement in the same publication.

Use testimonials. How many salespeople or businesses indicate that they are mediocre when they are trying to sell? Every advertising piece and sales pitch indicates how good they are (whether they are featuring price, service or added value). In the real world, our targets know that not everyone is excellent. They know this from experience. If you want to tell the world how great you are, then have a previous customer say it for you. A testimonial or third party endorsement has more impact than a self-serving statement.

Use guarantees. If you have a guarantee as part of your business and/or marketing plan, then feature this guarantee as part of your advertising. Make sure you can back your guarantee and that it differentiates you from the competition (see later within this chapter).

Achieve more than one objective. Our first synergy rule is to achieve two or more objectives through one action. Advertising uses our two most precious resources, time and money. We need to achieve as many results as possible every time we expend scarce resources. For example, if your call to action is broad enough, you can build your long-term prospect database as a result of your advertising efforts—in addition to achieving short-term sales.

Timing is important. The best advertising in the world will not work if the time is not right. On the other hand, the right timing can increase your advertising effectiveness significantly. The correct timing may depend upon a variety of cycles—including seasons, economic cycles, monthly cycles, purchase cycles and more. To determine your best timing you must know the purchase habits of your targets in the context of your product or service. Information concerning the advertising timing of your competitors will be very important as well. You may have to vary the timing of your advertising to determine the best combination for success.

Don't forget to sell. Advertising may make the phone ring, but only asking for the business and following up will make sales. You are wasting your money if you advertise but are too busy to answer the phone effectively or call people back.

Evaluation. It is said that the true definition of insanity is to do the same thing over and over and expect a different result. Consistency does not mean running the same advertisements when they are not achieving results. You must make adjustments in copy, offers, targets, timing and more. How many of us run the same advertisements over and over because we do not have the time to make a change? It is better not to advertise than to continue with something that will not help us achieve our goals in the long run. Ineffective actions rob us of our resources and create a false sense of accomplishment.

Articles—deliver real value

Articles represent an excellent way to market at little or no cost. They can be used in two ways:

- ◆ One may publish articles to gain name recognition and credibility. If you want to move to the forefront of your profession by being thought of as an expert, publishing is an excellent way to achieve this objective.
- ◆ One may provide articles (written by you or others) to your prospects, previous customers or other targets as a value-added activity.

With regard to publishing articles, it is important to note that name recognition and credibility are important. However, the laws of synergy marketing require that you achieve more than one objective from your activities. This means that the article should be designed to make the phone ring. You do this by utilizing a response mechanism that is basically an offer of value. I have written several columns for trade publications and my articles typically offer items for free. For example, if I write an article describing how to use customer service surveys, I might offer to provide a sample survey to those who call. Remember, credibility is important but making the phone ring gives you the opportunity to make a sale or develop a relationship.

It is also important to note that articles can be used again and again to achieve your goals. You may publish a particular article in a local newspaper. This does not preclude you also publishing the article in a trade journal—as long as the publications do not serve the same public. I have written articles that have appeared in up to ten publications and if I had been more aggressive, could have appeared in many, many more.

The same articles can also be integrated into your own newsletters that are then provided to your *sphere of influence* (see the sections on networking and newsletters). Of course, you can also offer reprints of the actual articles as a response mechanism rather than using the verbiage within the newsletter. Why write a newsletter from scratch if you have already written an article?

When providing articles to your sphere of influence, the use of articles published by your synergy marketing partners can provide the ultimate in synergistic activity. First, you are providing value to your network with little expenditure of resources because you did not have to write the article. Second, you are now providing value to your partner. Remember, providing this value puts you in a position to ask for something in return (the law of reciprocity).

Using an assistant

One of the most important rules of synergy marketing is to determine which tools are more effective than others. An assistant can certainly be considered a tool. You may have the best marketing plan in the world, but if you are spending your day stuffing envelopes and do not have the time to speak to customers as a result, you are unlikely to achieve your goals.

How can you tell if you need an assistant? If too much of your time is spent on tasks not directly related to the development of new business and/or you have been meaning to keep in touch with previous customers and cannot, this is a major indication of need.

Does having an assistant make you a manager? If you work for a large company, your assistant may not report to you. If you are a self-employed real estate or insurance agent, your assistant may be your employee (or an independent contractor who works with you). As a manager, you will be required to recruit and provide a job description for your assistant.

Do you have to hire someone to get it done? You may hire an individual or you might subcontract with a company to accomplish certain tasks. For example, instead of stuffing envelopes you might hire a mail house to do this for you. Instead of delivering flyers to offices, you might hire a flyer delivery firm. The important thing to determine is what tasks can be best accomplished by someone other than you and the most economical way to accomplish this "delegation" from the standpoint of time and money.

What can I delegate to my assistant? What you may delegate will vary depending upon your needs and the rules of your industry. In many disciplines—from real estate to stock brokerage—licensing regulations may limit the activities of assistants. Beyond the legalities, it is a good idea to determine what actions yield the greatest benefits in terms of the achievement of your long-term goals. In other words, what can the assistant undertake to free your time for more productive activities? The assistant may also help you in areas you are not proficient or do not like undertaking. For example, a salesperson not proficient with their computer may hire an assistant to specifically handle the automation activities of the office.

How do you determine your goals? There should be a direct relationship between how much you pay an assistant and how much your stress levels decrease and/or your income levels increase. If you cannot make this determination, you are unlikely to determine the effectiveness of a plan to hire an assistant.

How can I use synergy? There are many ways of integrating synergy into your plans for an assistant. The company or person you hire has a sphere of influence—can you exploit such to increase your own sphere? How can you set up the compensation schedule to reflect this goal? Perhaps you are a certified public accountant and you work closely with an estate attorney. Can you share mailing lists and the expenses necessary to subcontract the work? This may not only lower your costs, but also make you more aware of opportunities to add synergy to present actions.

Automation as a marketing tool

Tools are an important part of the sales process—and no tool is more important today than automation. Yet, as we are hurtling through the age of computers and the Internet, many are still not able to bring themselves into the 21st Century.

> *. . . Imagine approaching a new business tool. You are afraid of going near the contraption. You realize that it could save you some time, but just the same you are reticent to take the leap . . .*

Do you imagine that we are talking about your initial reluctance to embrace new technology in the form of fax machines just ten years ago? Try again. This is a description of the typical business person as they approached a new technology approximately 100 years ago—the stapler!

Imagine your newly acquired computer as a new version of a stapler. When your stapler does not work (anyone have one jam lately?) do you permanently abandon the technology in favor of paper clips, fix it or purchase a new stapler and start again? At some point you must accept this new technology. When you accept the computer and the Internet you will be on your way to success in the 21st Century.

Let us review some of the common tools available to us to reach our customers:

Telephones
Letters
Doorknobs
Advertisements

Now let us update each of these technologies:

The telephone becomes broadcast faxing or automated telemarketing;
The letter becomes direct mail;
The doorknob becomes e-mail; and,
The advertisement becomes the Internet.

How many of you are using these tools? Want to check your automation quotient? Do you have your e-mail and web address on your business card?

On the other hand, do you feel completely overwhelmed at hearing the words *RAM*, *megabyte*, *modem* or *Internet*? Do we sound like we are approaching maximum technobabble? Many small business owners and salespeople are completely lost within most automated systems. The question is: Do you need to automate to compete?

We think the answer to this question is yes, but with a resounding caution. No business person should automate for the sake of being automated. You must first ask yourself: To what problem does automation brings the most effective solution?

For example, perhaps your problem is keeping in touch with leads and previous customers. This includes sending letters (or e-mail), organizing contact information (including birthdays) and remembering your previous conversations. Perhaps your age old *sticky note* solution is just becoming untenable. The automated solution is contact management software. Using these programs, you can enter customer information and conversations, enable personalized communication and track correspondence.

The second question you must answer regards your own time and resources. Yes, there is an automated solution. Should you be effecting the solution, or is there a contract alternative? If you are going to use contact management software to effect large mailings, then perhaps you should contract with a direct mail house to handle the job. If you are interested in the custom graphics capability of publishing software, perhaps your printer can help rather than you becoming a graphics expert.

We say this because new automated systems can bring in-house most of the work you previously contracted out. But do you have the time? Each software system requires time for research, acquisition, training, testing and implementation. Will this time take you away from your main job, which is selling or perhaps recruiting? For too many sales professionals the computer has become a tool to enable our biggest handicap—call reluctance. If you cannot sell today because you are stuck on your computer, return to the first question and spend some time rethinking the automation process.

Leveraging the competition as your marketing tool

For most, the competition represents mythical figures possessing significant tactical and skill advantages over mere mortals such as ourselves. Every time we see evidence of our competition in action, we fantasize that their actions are more effective than they really are. Glorifying the competition is nothing new—sports coaches across the nation pump up their teams as they place their next opponents upon proverbial pedestals.

In reality, the competition represents mere mortals like us with a similar set of skills as everyone else. They also face the same problems we face each and every day. The grass is no greener on the other side. On the other hand, the grass is no less greener at our competitors' desks. Just putting our competition in perspective will help us proceed with one step that is essential within the sales process—*know thy competition*. Synergy dictates that some tools are more effective than others and there is no more effective tool than knowledge, especially with regard to your competition.

Why should we know our competition? We simply can be more effective as salespeople if we know the scope of our competitions' efforts. There is a multitude of information available regarding our competition that can be utilized to help us move up the ladder of success, such as:

- *Competitors' pricing levels.* We always think that we are being undercut by our competitors. Would you be surprised to know that they always believe that they are being undercut by us? The truth is that sometimes we beat our competition and sometimes we get beat by them. When your competitor runs a "special," do you know all the details and limitations? Sometimes you believe you are getting beat, but you are not.

- *Competitors' services.* Every salesperson provides a certain level of services to their clients—including those that are basic and those that they consider *value-added.* In addition to knowing their pricing structure, what services come with the basic package and what services are added to attract and keep additional customers? We also need to know how effective these added services are with regard to attracting additional business and building long-term loyalty.

- *The competitor from the customer's eyes.* Who are the major customers of your competitor and how do they view your competition? When customers utilize the competition, what strengths and weaknesses appear on a regular basis? Knowing your competition's strengths and weaknesses from your customers' eyes is much more important than seeing them from your own. This is why the sales process should always include questions that garner information regarding the present vendors (your competitors) of your prospects.

- *How does your competitor market?* What does your competitor do to attract business and how effective are those results? You may mistakenly conclude that the most visible efforts of your competitor (the efforts you are most likely to see) are the most effective. You may then emulate the wrong actions—a very expensive proposition. If you do that you would actually be working in reverse of the maximum synergy rules (using the least effective tools or marketing the least effective targets).

How do you extract information regarding your competition? Interviews with customers are an obvious method. Do not discount information gathered from your competition—directly and indirectly. In this day and age of the Internet, it is easier than ever to gather comprehensive information regarding your competitors. Indirectly, gather as much information as possible—advertisements, testimonials, etc.

Do not hesitate to ask a competitor to lunch. Your competition may well be as curious about you as you are about them. Benchmarking—the exchange of existing information—is a process that is used constantly by companies but not nearly enough by individual salespeople. You just might find out that your "bitter competition" may become your next great referral source. Imagine learning from your competition and also garnering referrals (not all companies handle all situations) at the same time. Does this sound like maximum synergy rule number one?

Just one hint: be prepared to give as much as you get through a direct meeting with your competitor. You cannot expect them to be forthright unless you make the same effort.

The result could be just what you need to be more effective in the long run. Imagine approaching a long-term sales target knowing who they use, why they use them and in what ways you can better their situation. You cannot effectively develop strategies to better the situations of your targets (needs assessments) unless you truly know the extent of value they are now receiving.

Using a database to deliver synergy

In today's computer world, we have made it easier for one to keep in touch with our sphere of influence. When you read the section on networking, you will note that one's sphere should range from several hundred to a few thousand individuals. If you are networking properly, there is no way that you can keep in touch with your sphere using a *sticky note* system.

And keeping in touch with your sphere will be more and more important as companies become larger and technology becomes more sophisticated. Larger companies have larger customer bases. In other words, if you don't keep in touch with your customers, someone else will.

Whether you procure your own contact management software or hire a database management company (they used to be called mailing houses), there are a few basic rules:

- ◆ The database must be organized to identify certain groups (the networking section describes this process in detail).
- ◆ Certain information must be entered in a way that will allow for future activities, ranging from simple birthday reminders to the expiration dates of investments requiring sales maintenance activities.
- ◆ You must be able to use your database to actively reach your sphere in more than one way—mailing, e-mailing and faxing. If you have

important news (such as announcing tax law changes), you may need to be able to provide this value more quickly than your normal mode of communication.

◆ You must be able to enter contact information (such as call logs) that will help you later in the sales process. For example, if the target mentions that he/she is taking a trip to Europe next summer and you speak to them next October, you should be able to note the earlier conversation so you can ask how the trip went. This is how relationships are built. I will attest to the fact that automatic memories work much better than the human mind as one attains a certain age!

◆ You should be constantly utilizing your marketing activities to build-up the contents of your database. For example, a response mechanism within your website should be designed to result in one or more points of contact that will add prospects to your database. If you do not do this on a consistent basis you will be wasting a synergy opportunity.

Once you have created an effective database you have created an important asset. You can now leverage that asset through reciprocal relationships with synergy marketing partners. By accomplishing a joint mailing to both databases you can double or triple the size of your list overnight. This is a simple example of adding additional doses of synergy to your marketing actions.

Obviously, there are many uses of your database as a facilitator of the implementation of marketing activities. These activities will be discussed throughout this book—from the provision of newsletters to direct mail. None of them can be implemented effectively without a complete database. This is an essential tool for any business and will become even more essential in the future.

Direct mail marketing

Technology is advancing so quickly it is a surprise direct mail is still a part of the sales process. Today we are just as likely to use the Internet, e-mail or broadcast faxes to reach our clients. With so many ways of reaching consumers, it is even more imperative that whatever marketing efforts we chose to utilize, they must be as effective as possible.

In other words, if we are going to use direct mail we better be effective. The other choices are to do nothing (and to achieve nothing) or to mail without knowing whether your mailings could be achieving significantly more impact. We will focus our treatment of this topic within the following general categories: objectives, targets, timing, uniqueness, simplicity, the offer, response mechanisms, consistency, performance evaluation and change.

Start with a measurable objective. Many mail with the idea that they would like to *keep their name in front of their customers.* We will call this the objective of *visibility.* While visibility, as well as similar objectives such as *name identification* and *credibility* are viable goals, they don't lead to measurable results. We love name identification, but can't eat name identification. We only eat when the phone rings with substantive client response. If your direct mail is not making the phone ring, it is a poor use of your limited resources.

Synergy marketing begins with an all important rule: every marketing activity must achieve two results. Why can't your direct mail achieve credibility, keep your name in front of previous customers and make your phone ring at the same time?

Of course, measuring how many times your phone rings is one thing. Measuring the achievement of your final result is another. If your phone rings constantly because of your mailing efforts and you do not achieve the results intended, there are two possible explanations.

The first explanation regards conversion. After your direct mail does its job, you must then rely upon your telephone skills. If your telephone skills are poor, then you will receive little benefit from the calls received.

Reach the correct target. The second explanation regards your intended target. If your phone rings but the wrong group is responding, you will not achieve any perceivable objectives. As a matter of fact, if your target is wrong you might never receive any response at all and it may be that you will never know if the direct mail you are sending was ineffective or the intended audience was off-target.

Sometimes the appropriateness of the target list is obvious. For example, mailing to your previous customers is almost always appropriate because this list represents the target group with which you have the strongest relationship. This is not to say that the material or timing is always appropriate. On the other hand, targeting prospects with whom you don't have a relationship is much more complex. Your list may correspond to one of several categories:

◆ Geographic targets;

◆ Demographics—such as income;

◆ Employment data;

◆ Relationship with a marketing partner—someone else's list;

◆ Respondents to other offers—attendees of a seminar;

◆ Interests—such as golfing enthusiasts;

◆ Ownership status–such as investor properties; and,

◆ Debt status—mortgage or credit histories.

This list is not intended to be inclusive; just to demonstrate the many ways one might target a mailing or other marketing campaign. Of course, these categories may be combined and/or further subdivide to present a more precise targeted approach. One such example would be to target owners of investment properties within a certain zip code. The further one stray's from intimate relationships, the more important it is to pinpoint and match your target and your objectives with pristine accuracy.

Of course, you might mail to the right target with the right piece and still not achieve your objectives. One explanation for the lack of response would be a poor sense of timing.

Timing is everything in life. We can mail to the right targets but if we mail at the wrong time we will receive little or no results. Some of the issues regarding timing are quite simple. For example, mailing before the Christmas Holidays when mail is the heaviest is not a good idea in most cases. If you are trying to reach the business person who is using the Holiday quiet period to clean out their desk, then you may be on target for an end of the year mailing.

Other timing issues are much more complex. It would not be untypical for a real estate professional to mail to apartment complexes in order to target first time homebuyers. This is a great tactic that can be made even better by further refining the target to include those with good credit, stable jobs, etc. Mailing before the Spring homebuying season might constitute a good plan. What might constitute even a better idea is to mail right after the apartment complex announces an increase in rent. Tenants always think about purchasing a home in the weeks after receiving such a notice. What a great time for a letter describing how they are making their landlord rich. If you wait 30 days to mail the urge will have faded.

CPA's might mail before tax season hits, and directly after W-2's are mailed. Those mailing for home equity/debt consolidation loans know that there is no time like mailing after the first credit card bills are received subsequent to the holidays. We could continue with an endless string of examples, but the point is simple. It is easy to see that we could be mailing to the right target at the wrong time and therefore not achieve our objectives.

You better be unique. Uniqueness is the cornerstone of marketing—and without this facet you will be missing a major component of synergy. Major corporations—FedEx, Dominos, McDonalds—were built and became successful because they were unique. Today's consumers and business people are receiving so many pieces of direct mail, e-mails, faxes and telemarketing calls that it is imperative now more than ever to be unique. It has gotten so competitive that what used to be deemed unique is now run of the mill.

Take a gander at your mail today. You have envelopes that look like they contain U.S. Treasury checks. Other envelopes appear to come as *urgent overnight delivery.* Still others make it appear as if you are one of only four finalists who have won two million dollars. They then sneak in a plain envelope that looks handwritten—no return address. You are sure to open this last attempt because you don't know if it could be from a personal friend.

No offense to the marketing gurus of the world, but when the average consumer receives ten of these each day they end up in the garbage—usually unopened. So with all the bells and whistles looking like another bunch of junk mail, how can you be unique? Try partnering up with people/companies with whom your target has a relationship. For example, if a company is served by a software vendor, they are likely to open any communication that comes from that company. Perhaps the piece contains news concerning an update to their program.

If a letter comes from their accountant, software company or even their bank they are likely to open the letter and read the contents. If the letter is written by someone with which they have a relationship, they are even more likely to act upon the offer. This is called a third-party endorsement. Fancy envelopes are easier, but less effective than partnership endeavors. Six page letters with 14 offers are eye catching, but not as effective as plain simple talk about benefits from someone they know and trust.

Simplicity. The world continues to become more and more complex. Our prospects are receiving stimuli from thousands of sources. What a refreshing change it is for them to receive a mailing that is simple, easy to understand and painless for them to fashion a response! Wasn't it Lee Iacocca who once said:

> *"Tell them what you are going to say,*
> *say it and then tell them what you said."*

There is no doubt that those who send two and three page direct mailings with two or three inserts have lost sight of this worthy goal. The average American consumer—if they were so inclined to spend the time—could not figure out what the offer was, how it benefited them and how they could respond with a minimum amount of time and energy expended. Examine your last direct mail piece and compare this to a few received in the mail within the past week. Just how simple are they compared to yours?

This is not to say that you will sell a $5,000 product with a two sentence postcard. The sales pitch must fit the situation. Are you looking for the letter to entice the customer to respond or make a final decision on the product or service? If you are aiming for a warm lead, the pitch can be brief.

There are a few important simplicity rules. Start with the benefits to the consumer—or the pain they might be avoiding—within the first paragraph. Make sure the response mechanism is located within the first page—or there is only one page. Use short paragraphs and highlight important points. Can it be read in less than 30 seconds? If not, you have lost the average consumer! Finally, make sure the prospect will easily understand the action you would like them to take. If they have to think about how to respond, the best offer in the world will be lost.

The offer. The offer is one area most direct mail efforts seem to have down pat. Most direct mailings contain an offer right on the envelope: $20,000 spending money—quick! The offer is meant to get the envelope opened. And then the consumer finds out how accurate the offer really is. Do you remember the last time you received a sweepstakes mailing? Didn't it seem as though you had won—until you opened the envelope?

Making the offer prominent is a good idea. Do not follow with making your target disappointed by opening the letter. Make the offer simple, on target, enticing and realistic. The secret of great sales is exceeding your customers' expectations. If you promise more than you can deliver you will never exceed your customers' expectations. The secret of great direct mail efforts is to get your targets to respond—not to get them to expect something you can't possibly deliver most of the time. The offer is an important synergy tool—if used correctly.

Response mechanisms. Response is best achieved through a targeted response mechanism. The best direct mail offers receive responses from far less than one out of every 100 targets. Most are closer to one out of 1,000. The goal of your direct mail effort is to get the target to contact your company. If their reason for response is so limited that very few will pick up the phone, you have wasted two major resources—time and money.

On the other hand, if you have the ability to entice four or five times as many responses, there will be many more sales opportunities. Offering mortgages to those with bad credit will get response. Offering a free article regarding choosing credit counseling services will get a wider response. The response mechanism can be separate from your main offer. The purpose of the mailing is to get your phone to ring with the most amount of respondents who could use your services. If you are ready to sell over the phone, you will find many sales opportunities.

Response mechanisms should not be limited to direct mail efforts. Every contact with the public—from your voice mail to newspaper advertisements—should contain an enticing response mechanism. The best tools will increase your responses many times over.

Visualize what you would like them to see. The piece must be visually appealing in some way. If the type is too small, those over 45 years of age may have a hard time reading the material. There are many other aspects to visualization. For example, odd numbers ($683) can be more believable than even numbers (over $650). The important points must stand-out and yet the material must not look like a circus—therefore you should make judicious use of headlines and a "P.S." The tone should be personal and not written as if it applies to the 10,000 targets.

Consistency and Evaluation. When asked how effective direct mail efforts seem to be, we usually receive one of two answers:

- We tried a direct mail piece, but it did not work; or,
- We have been mailing for some time but we don't know how well it is working.

Let us first address the first response. Tried direct mail? Mailing one or two times to an important constituency such as your previous customers is not likely to receive immediate and measurable impact. A one-time effort lacks a major characteristic of direct mail success—consistency. One mails to develop long-term relationships with previous customers and to have this group think of you each time they have a need for your services. Long-term relationships are not developed with one transaction and they are not developed with a one-time mail effort.

It is true that one mailing can receive response—especially if the timing is right and there is a decent offer and response mechanism. However, you are not likely to achieve long-term impact without a long-term, consistent direct mail strategy. Without this strategy, you are likely to receive hit and miss results.

What long-term strategies might one employ? With previous customers the strategy might be as simple as consistent contact on significant dates such as anniversaries of automobile purchases. The strategy also might be complex, working in the consistent development of value-added strategies such as the provision of tax information to your customers' accountants at the beginning of tax season or targeted articles on the state of the market during certain economic cycles.

The second situation described regards the lack of knowledge of the efficacy of one's direct mail efforts. If one does not realize the value of their efforts and continues to put forth these efforts, are they wise or insane? Why would someone not realize the value of their efforts? Perhaps they are busy and cannot measure from where the business is coming. We will call this the case of the *sloppy marketer*. The salesperson is happy because business is rolling, so why question the efforts? Sales are helping fuel the marketing efforts (money is being made), resources are adequate to maintain the status quo and we really don't have the time for in-depth analysis.

For many of those accomplishing the marketing, we have to be much more judicious with our resources. In other words, if the direct mail campaigns are not contributing to the bottom line we just can't afford to continue the efforts. So why do we?

We must not confuse consistency with effectiveness. Mailing consistently does not at all denote that we must mail to the same targets with the same goals and the same material over and over again. Consistency means that we must attack our goals from various angles before achieving a desired result. If one piece does not work, try a different tack. This different tack might include changing the target, timing, offer, response mechanism or any other part of the direct mail efforts.

True evaluation of your efforts requires measurement of the results. How many phone calls were generated by the piece? How many of these calls were converted into appointments or referrals? If your phone is ringing and the appointments are not occurring, there may not be a problem with direct mail but your telephone skills. Are your conversion rates consistent with other top producers receiving similar calls? Yes, measurement of the results requires an extra step and will utilize your most precious resource—time. The alternative is spending even more of your resources—time and money—possibly for little or no gain. It may be even worse not to realize from where the results are coming. If the market were to slow and resources became tight, where would you focus these scarcities?

All marketing efforts including direct mail must be agents of change. Every aspect that we have discussed has the ability to be fluid. It is those who change with market cycles who will become market leaders of tomorrow. Think about current population trends and how our targets have changed in the past ten years. So before you mail, get ready to try and try again.

E-mail instead of snail mail

In the computer age there is no avoiding the fact that we will have to use e-mail to achieve our business objectives. E-mail may be a tool that can be used for several different functions within the area of business development.

◆ Direct solicitation of potential clients (a substitution of direct mail or faxing);
◆ Setting up appointments with potential clients (elimination of voice mail *tag*); and,
◆ Delivery of proposals or customer service information.

Indeed, the use of e-mail can carry advantages over traditional methods of communication (telephones and direct mail). For one thing, e-mails are less expensive to send in bulk than direct mail. E-mails also represent a quick and effective method of communication enabling one to keep others informed (copying function) quite easily.

E-mails also have some very important disadvantages. For one, they are easy to ignore—especially if the e-mail is unsolicited. With e-mail "spamming" rampant and headlines of deadly viruses, it is quite possible that one may hit the delete button before opening an e-mail if it does not originate clearly from their close contacts or pertain to their personal interest. Direct mail may come in very elaborate packaging designed to entice the target to open the solicitation. With e-mail, one must open the communication to view the packaging.

Speaking of packaging, the format of e-mails must be much simpler than other forms of written communication. There is no way to standardize the format in a way that the e-mail will appear exactly on your machine the same as it will appear on the receiver's machine. We have previously indicated that advertising messages must be very simple. In the case of e-mails, the message and the package must be extraordinarily simplistic.

One method of expanding the format of e-mails is to attach more elaborate documents (such as "Word" or "PDF" documents). However, adding this step will lessen the probability that the message will be fully viewed because of caution (viruses) and expediency (the time necessary to download such files). This also assumes the entity in receipt possesses the software program needed to open the attachment.

Despite these disadvantages, anyone can attest to the fact that e-mail solicitations are proliferating exponentially over the Internet. Forrester Research predicts that spending on e-mail marketing will reach $4.8 billion by 2004. Systems such as closed business Intranet systems may be able to more effectively block such mass solicitations, yet the practice will continue to grow and firewalls are constantly broken. As the use of this tool grows so will the sophistication of marketing and formatting techniques. It remains to be seen whether e-mail will effectively replace direct mail or telephone as a major method of mass marketing.

Aside from mass marketing, there is no doubt that e-mails can be an effective marketing tool on an individual level. Sending an e-mail to introduce yourself to an potential target may be an effective way of *softening the call*. This may well be an important part of the process known as "warming-up the cold call." E-mails will add another point of contact to letters, faxes and phone calls when attempting to establish recognition in preparation for a first "face-to-face" meeting.

E-mails also help tremendously within the customer service function. Delivering great customer service is often determined by how well you communicate. E-mail gives you an easy and convenient way to communicate within the sales and operational processes. For example, if you have a preferred customer base at a retail clothing store, you can let your personal clients know when there is a sale coming up. If you are an investment advisor and the stock you recommended had a great day, you can send an e-mail. If you have an approval process (for example, mortgages), you can give status on the process.

Nothing substitutes for great communication and e-mail gives us another tool within our communication arsenal. Of course, it is up to us to use it effectively. It is in this regard that the use of synergy becomes essential. E-mail gives us another method of delivering value to our customer base. It also represents another way to integrate our marketing efforts with our synergy partners. If you have amassed a marketing list through a response mechanism on your Internet site, it would be quite easy to solicit this list in the name of a synergy partner while they do the same to their list on your behalf. For confidentiality purposes the e-mail to your list advertising your partner would be sent from your company (and vice-versa). The inexpensive nature of e-mail marketing enables this to become an important method of leveraging your assets as you add blocks of synergy to present activities.

Endorsements or testimonials or social proof— we call them total synergy

Credibility and trust. Selling is a relationship business and without these key elements any salesperson will be struggling in the dark trying to overcome an enormous handicap. What do you say when a potential seller or purchaser asks the key question:

Why should I do business with you?

Do you think that anyone has answered that question with the truth if the salesperson in question does not return phone calls or is generally poorly educated and/or prepared? The standard answer is:

Because I am a great _____ and I will do a great job!

Think of your potential customer or client as a potential employer. Do you think anyone a company interviews admits that they will show up for work late constantly and will generally perform poorly? Yet, how many people have you seen hired by a company do just that?

So the question remains, how are you going to get that person to trust your answer to this statement? The most effective way is to have someone else (preferably several *someone elses*) say that you are good instead of you tooting your own horn. There is nothing more powerful than a third-party recommendation.

When your previous customer, a vendor and/or even one of their neighbors states that they would not go wrong by hiring you, there is very little that you can add that will boost your cause any further. Does this mean that you must get several people to call before a presentation or bring an entourage with you? Of course not! The most effective means of third-party referrals is the *referral letter*.

You see referral letters everywhere. Next time you bring your car into service at a new car dealership, peruse the bulletin board. Quotes from satisfied customers become powerful segments of advertisements when you receive fliers asking you to try a product or attend a seminar.

How do you obtain more referral letters? Of course, the easiest solution is to ask for them. Many of us do not even bother to follow-up after a transaction, let alone secure a letter from a satisfied customer. Calling a customer after the transaction is far from our only solution.

One place to look for referral letters is among your vendors. These people should be motivated to help you—or they should not be your vendor. Do you think that a letter from a professional will not have as much of an impact as a satisfied customer? Think again—these players handle hundreds of transactions and are considered experts. Just make sure to coach them on pointing this fact out:

> *"I have been a settlement agent in the real estate business*
> *for ten years and have been involved in over a*
> *thousand transactions and Mary Smith is . . ."*

The second way to boost your portfolio with solid referral letters is to use a customer satisfaction survey. It is true that many people just won't sit down and write a letter, no matter how many times you ask. The only solution for these people is to obtain a quote from them verbally and type up the letter for their signature (not a bad solution—anything that gets the job done!) or to provide them with a fill-in-the-blank alternative such as a survey.

A follow-up survey can provide valuable information in addition to referral letters. You can learn about areas for improvement and also can use the opportunity to ask for referrals. Just asking whether they would refer you to someone else is not enough—leave a blank to fill in a name. The effective use of customer service surveys or evaluations is a prime example of synergy marketing rule number one—achieving more than one objective from one action. This characteristic makes them a very effective marketing tool (rule number four).

Be sure to leave plenty of space when asking for a general opinion of your service. Each positive quote becomes a referral letter. To increase your response rate even further, bring the survey to them personally and have them complete it immediately. Another idea to increase your rate of response is to offer an incentive of some kind. The incentive may be something of value from your synergy marketing partner.

Now when you go to a presentation you can be armed with five, ten or even a hundred referral letters. Put the quotes together in a flyer and don't forget to use actual names. Anonymous quotes are not as effective. Use the quotes in every mailing and newspaper advertisement within your arsenal and even on your fax cover sheets. How can you be more effective than presenting with an army of people at your side?

Faxing—here today and gone tomorrow?

Never before has a tool been more representative of the fast-paced changing world of technology than fax transmissions. In the early 1980s, fax machines were slow and had poor transmission quality. Overall, they were light-years ahead of the mail service (even FedEx was new in those days) in terms of arriving instantly as opposed to overnight or in a few days. I helped manage a Congressional Office during this period and delivering the text for speeches out in the district from the Washington office was an important tool—even if delivery took several minutes for each page. How did we ever live without such an important technology?

As we moved into the 1990s, thermal paper was replaced by plain paper and ink-jets were replaced by lasers. Faxing quality and speed was improved tremendously. The ability to "broadcast" fax to hundreds or thousands of numbers simultaneously moved fax technology from an important business tool to an important marketing tool.

While this transition was taking place, the Internet and e-mails became viable means of mass-communication and have given the business world another alternative at a time in which faxing could have become a more popular alternative to direct mail. While faxing carries advantages over direct mail in terms of cost (though it is not as inexpensive as emails) and instant delivery, there are also several disadvantages:

- ◆ Faxing is basically a business-to-business marketing tool. While more homes have fax receipt capability, home faxing is not an established marketing method.
- ◆ Faxing has a more intrusive quality than direct mail and e-mail. Direct mail can be thrown out without opening the envelope and e-mail can be deleted without opening the communication. Faxing uses the paper of the recipient and ties up the machine and can prevent outgoing and incoming transmissions. In addition, with the growth of home businesses, many business fax machines are located in the home and transmission at night (for lower phone

rates) can produce some very irate responses.

- Fax graphics quality, while more controllable than e-mails, will never be the equivalent of direct mail. You cannot fax color and you cannot control the quality of the receiving machine.
- Delivery of faxes can be uneven. If the "receiving machine" is tied up or other wise out of commission, the fax will not be sent. Redials can happen only so many times.

These disadvantages not withstanding, faxing can be an important tool within a business-to-business marketing or customer service plan. For example, wholesale mortgage lenders regularly use fax technology to inform their mortgage brokers of their daily rates—though the Internet may replace this function in the long run. These everyday uses allow us opportunities to utilize maximum synergy rules to increase our marketing effectiveness.

For example, are your fax cover sheets designed to sell? As a national speaker, I placed my list of programs and speaking schedule on the background on every fax cover sheet. The cover sheet already exists, why not utilize it to its full advantage? Your value proposition or guarantee can be printed on these sheets. As we have indicated within the previous section—so can your testimonials. How can your synergy marketing partners take advantage of your regular faxing to a large list? For example, you fax may be offering value via an item from a partner. This way you deliver value to your target and your partner. With one activity!

Using a guarantee as part of the plan

Guarantees are common marketing tools within the business world. Major corporations have built their empires around guarantees to the general public—

- Dominos guaranteed delivery at 30 minutes or less.
- Several retail chains advertise some variation of: *we will not be undersold* (adding the refund of the difference plus ten percent).
- Real estate companies have experimented with *guaranteed sale price* for listings.
- Hotel chains and restaurants have *satisfaction* guarantees.

If used correctly, a guarantee can be a powerful tool to assure the public or business customers regarding the strength of the offer and/or service of your company. It can be used as part of a multi-million dollar marketing campaign or an individual offer to a particular customer. As a matter of fact, I can remember giving my personal guarantee of service to garner a particular customer as an originator in the mortgage business. If you peruse the literature of marketing guru, Dan Kennedy, his programs always offer a guarantee of some kind.

In order for guarantees to be effective you should abide by the following rules:

- *Don't promise if you cannot deliver.* The worst position you can put yourself in is not delivering consistently on a guarantee. Your reputation will become much worse if you raised expectations and then fall short on a consistent basis. Understand what you guarantee and what you cannot guarantee. For example, if you are an attorney you can guarantee that you will have the paperwork filed on time, but you may not be able to guarantee that you will win the case for your client.

- *Have a specific remedy as part of a guarantee.* What do you do if the customer is not satisfied? I have noticed at times that certain hotels specify guaranteed satisfaction, but to not specify what they will do if you are not satisfied.

- *If you do fall short, do not argue.* Much of the good publicity is gained through backing the guarantee. As a matter of fact, I have known certain individuals to "miss the mark" at the beginning of a guarantee promotion . . . on purpose. They pay off on the guarantee in a very public way—so that the public knows that they are serious. For years, the Hershman Group has given a 30-day return guarantee on all products (books, tapes, newsletters) and has backed that guarantee with a "no-argument" policy. In implementing this policy, we many times find that if someone is not happy with a particular product, it is because they expected something else and that "something else" may be filled through another product offering. In other words, those who would like to take advantage of the guarantee may actually present an opportunity to effect another sale and produce a satisfied customer—if you listen.

- *Understand that the majority of the public will not take advantage.* The most important effect of the guarantee is piece of mind— it makes your clients feel good. Many will not even check on the price because they feel you would not make the claim if you were not competitive. In other words, do not shy from guarantees because you feel your customers will besiege you with bogus demands. Some will take advantage, but the majority will not.

◆ *Make your guarantee part of your long-term business plan.* The guarantee should not exist to gain a burst of publicity or produce short-term results—it should be part of a plan to achieve your long-term goals. If the guarantee is for service—such as returning phone calls the same day—then it should be part of your long-term plan for customer service. Why is returning calls promptly important and how will it help you achieve your long-term goals? Why do you want to be known as the company that returns calls promptly and how will that differentiate yourself from the competition?

In the long run, the guarantee can become more than a useful marketing tool. It can become a part of your long-term business plan and business brand identification. If you use this tool, you must be judicious in the application, marketing and implementation of the guaranteed results. It should be part of your marketing plan and it must be applied consistently to make a long-term difference. Guarantees do not make good short-run promotions because you do not create identities in the short run.

Headlines—make them stand up and take notice

Headlines are an important part of marketing because of the basic premise upon which this book is predicated. We are stressed because we do not have enough time to implement our marketing, sales and management programs. If we do not have enough time to take marketing actions, what makes you think that our targets have enough time to receive our marketing and sales efforts? Of course, they don't.

This is why sales training is constantly trying to help us regarding how to get in front of our customers when they do not have time. We need to learn how to get someone on the phone, how to get an appointment and how to keep their attention for more than 30 seconds.

Headlines are important because the average recipient of our marketing material may do no more than read the headline. If the headline does not grab their interest in some way, they will not read any further. Because of this, marketing literature is interspersed with advice on how to deliver "attention grabbing" headlines. *Cash Copy* by Dr. Jeffrey Lant (JLA Publications, 1989) gives a great overall treatment of how copy can help grab the attention of your prospects and help instill in them the will to take action.

Headlines must grab the attention of the prospects, but they must not do so with a promise that is so outrageous that the prospect will be disappointed a few sentences later. The adage that we cannot promise more than we can deliver applies to the whole sales process as well as your advertising copy. As someone involved in the education and training of the business world, I take particular umbrage to seminar headlines that read *"Double Your Production."* If goals are achieved in small increments (Kaizen), then how is someone with 20 years in sales going to double their production in a three hour seminar? And how is the presenter going to exceed their expectations—are they going to have the participants triple their production?

Headlines can accent negative or positive consequences. Some in advertising believe that the focus upon preventing a negative has a more significant psychological impact than hyping positive results. Here are a few examples of negatives headlines focusing upon the elimination or prevention of negative situations:

No More Cold-Calling

Keep The Banks From Owning Your House

Don't Let The IRS Profit From Your Labor

Here are some examples of headlines with a positive focus:

Get Ready For the Technological Revolution

Earn More Money in Less Time

Maximum Synergy—More Productivity With Less Stress

In other words, this book is an example of proposing a positive result rather than emphasizing the negative of not reading this book. We could have focused upon the negative with this catchy title:

Prevent The Time Bomb of Stress From Wrecking Your Productivity

The distinction is clear. What you need to find out is what is going to motivate your prospects into taking action—without becoming so grandiose in your promises that your prospects will become disappointed after taking this action. Because if they are disappointed they will not become long-term customers and you will continue to have to produce more and more new prospects every year. This is truly a time bomb of stress and it can wreck more than your productivity.

The Internet and your marketing plan

It is a fact that the Internet age has now arrived. Just watch television and see how many dot.com commercials appear. Consumers are booking vacations, buying cars, obtaining mortgages and going grocery shopping on-line. Though the technology slump of 2000-2001 has slowed the momentum, there is no doubt that on-line marketing will be part of all industry's marketing efforts in the future.

All markets will be affected by the Internet age. To compete, we must first decide how we can get involved so we can increase our possibilities of success while not taking away from our other marketing efforts? Where does one go from here?

We must decide what we want to accomplish through the Internet. Is the Internet going to be the major thrust of your marketing efforts or provide support for your overall marketing plan? Is the Internet going to be one of our five vehicles for advertising—or is it the only marketing effort? Is your target businesses or the consumer? It is obviously easier to reach a specific business via the Internet than it is to target the whole world.

Advertising. Yes, there are millions and millions of people surfing the web— but there are almost as many sites. Imagine a mall that big; how hard would it be to find a particular store? In July of 1999, it was reported that there were more than 50 million web pages relevant to home mortgages (*National Mortgage Broker*, August, 1999). People searching for sites may find thousands within their geographic area and/or selling the same product. You must advertise to drive people to your site.

This does not mean that you must take out full-page ads in newspapers advertising that you have a web site. It does mean that every marketing piece you produce must include a feature of your website address—from your business cards to newspaper advertisements. You may be surprised to find how many shoppers will visit or call you only after viewing the information on the net first.

Signing up for all the "search engines" in the world will not replace your own marketing plan (though search engines are obviously important factors in the web "search" process). If the net represents a significant part of your marketing efforts, then a greater part of your resources should be spent advertising your site.

Links. Not all advertising of your web site must cost money. The best way to drive people to your site in a cost effective manner is to utilize your synergy marketing partners. Think of all the vendors you utilize and other relationships you have developed. Do any of them have a web site? Would they allow you to show a link from their site to yours? Be prepared to reciprocate and the links from your site to your partners' represent an additional marketing opportunity. Now the browser will be able to find a multitude of services by visiting your site. Your site can become a virtual mall for your particular industry.

It is here that you can make maximum use of synergy. If you spend time putting together interesting and useful content for a site—for example, an accountant might publish ten alternatives to reduce your tax burden—why not offer this content to your synergy marketing partners? Instead of merely a link, the partners could use your content to upgrade the substance of their site and you obtain free advertising for your site.

Make them stay. Thus far we have spent our time talking about how to drive people to the site ("hits" in web speak). Once there, the effort will be worthless unless they want to stay. Your site should be attractive and interesting. It should also be easy to navigate. Do not hesitate to add a personal touch, such as a picture of your staff. Your site may very well be your company's first impression to the majority of the public.

Make them stick. Attract traffic to the site, make them use the site and then make them want to make contact and come back. What good is spending a significant amount of resources if you receive no benefit? Perhaps they do not see a product for sale to their liking—what will make them contact you in any case instead of merely moving to the next site?

One method of doing this is to offer a response mechanism (synergy marketing rule number 6) that represents something of value to the browser. There must be something that will prod the browser to take action, i.e. contacting you through the site or by phone. *Our synergy rules indicate that you only make money if the phone rings.* What could this thing of value be? Perhaps it is an article that will help them prepare for retirement, a brochure on the tax benefits of owning investment property, a subscription to a news-letter or a special offer from a synergy partner with a link through your site.

Other means of keeping people engrossed in your site include changing content (for example monthly articles or news service links), increasing credibility through advertising your successes and testimonials and making them feel comfortable with your value proposition, perhaps through a guarantee. Your site is a means of advertising and the general rules of advertising apply.

Follow-up. Once you drive traffic to the site and receive responses, the most important step is follow-up. In most industries, few will contract for your services without some sort of personal contact. It doesn't have to be "pushy." Call to ask whether they enjoyed the article and see whether there is something else you can do for them. If they are not ready to move, ask if they know anyone else who could use your services. Referrals are obtained only one way—*by asking.*

Networking as a marketing tool—cold calling revisited

In several instances we have intimated that cold calling is not the most effective way to produce increased business. Within the chapter that focuses upon sales skills, Lynne Waymon enlightens us with ideas as to how to network. Here we delve into a more detailed example of how to use our sphere of influence to organize an important network as a base of business as opposed to cold calling.

We have been taught again and again that the key to being successful in sales is the development of relationships. If this is true, then why do sales trainers and sales managers spend so much time trying to teach cold calling skills?

◆ In real estate, we cold call neighborhoods;
◆ In the mortgage business, we visit real estate offices;
◆ Stock brokerages are known for calling from a phone book (though the practice has been tempered in recent years);
◆ Telemarketing operations have flourished in recent years, with private residences being called constantly.

Pick up the phone and make a call. Some believe that we are proving our mettle by demonstrating an ability to *"beat the streets."* We have another word for this professional behavior—*stupid.*

Why is cold calling stupid? Simply stated, if we have to utilize our most precious resource—time—in an effort to meet people for the first time over and over again, we will be running on a treadmill for the rest of our lives. As a matter of fact, the practice of cold calling may be a major factor as to why the profession of sales is a revolving door. If you look at sales personnel in almost every field there is a major issue with turnover.

If cold calling is not the way to succeed in sales, what is the alternative? Call people you know! Ask yourself before you pick up the phone to cold call: have you contacted every one you know in order to achieve your sales goals? Are your marketing efforts designed to produce warm leads through the maximum synergy rules and have you linked your telemarketing efforts to fully exploit these warm leads before you begin to cold call? We believe that most people have at least 300 personal contacts within the following groups:

- ◆ Personal—friends, relatives, neighbors;
- ◆ Associations—religious organizations, civic associations, the PTA;
- ◆ Previous customers—from this job or a previous place of employment;
- ◆ Previous prospects—contacts you were not able to sell in the past;
- ◆ Coworkers—from this job or a previous place of employment;
- ◆ Professionals—doctors, CPA's, attorneys; and,
- ◆ Vendors—those who call on your industry and/or your targets.

We challenge you to sit down at a computer and come up with a personal contact list using this format. We believe that when you have finished a thorough exercise, the estimation of three to five hundred contacts will be conservative. If you do not have a working database, you now have started the basis for one. If you do have a working database, your database will now be stronger.

The question remains: If you have 300 or more personal contacts, why would you call someone you do not know in order to sell? One common response to this question is that you do not want to sell those you know. This response represents a type of call reluctance and has been addressed in the appropriate section of this book.

Many assume that their personal contacts will automatically refer them business when it is available. This is a very false assumption. Your contacts do not sit around and think about who they know and what they do for a living and act accordingly. They usually act under the *"path of least resistance theory."* This means that the person who contacted them most recently from the time a need occurred is most likely to be the conduit for new business. The way to interfere with this process is to develop really close relationships. Yes, sales really is relationships.

Top producers in every field of sales obtain the majority of their business from referrals. Their greatest source of referrals are those with whom they have developed a close relationship—especially previous customers. If you have not kept in touch with those you have served in the past, you are likely to have to start the sales process from scratch every time you have to make another sale. Talk about a treadmill!

Let us take a look at each of these categories more carefully.

Personal contacts. The first, *personal contacts,* may seem to be the least complex. Everyone has relatives, friends and neighbors within their sphere of influence. Many business-to-business entities do not market to individuals but rather target companies—both large and/or small. The business niche of your company may be very specific, yet it should not be assumed that our closest individual contacts cannot be a part of our marketing plan. All companies are comprised of individuals.

Many times individual salespeople are reticent to call upon those who are the closest to them. Perhaps they feel they will appear not to be "doing well" in front of those who care about them the most. This phenomenon represents a common form of call reluctance. It should be noted that those who are *succeeding* are the ones most likely to make their personal network an important source of referrals.

Some businesses make personal contacts a major part of the marketing plan. For example, real estate agents are known for mailing to or "farming" their local area. It is not unusual for a real estate professional to advertise themselves as the "neighborhood" Realtor®.

Let us suppose you are a real estate agent and you are invited to dinner at a neighbor's house. When you arrive, there is a new *for sale* sign. And it is not yours. As a matter of fact, it is a perfect stranger who does not live in the neighborhood. How do you feel? Did you expect your neighbor to think of you when you did not spend any time asking them for their business or referrals? Never assume they will think of you on their own.

Associations. The *Association* category covers a wide range of organized groups—personal, religious, civic and business. Today, it is not unusual for someone to be involved in their church or temple, a professional association and their children's PTA or school sports.

Every member of these associations represents a possible marketing target or referral source. Your actions could include simply advertising in the association newsletter or e-mailing to close members. Perhaps you might take a leadership role in the association, that would enable you to become known by more members. Certainly networking at association events is an opportunity of which every member can avail themselves. Of course, this means that you must become active by attending these meetings and actually networking (bring your business cards).

Networking does not mean walking around and asking for the business (or plastering the room with business cards). It does mean asking others what they do for a living, in turn making them obligated to ask you the same question. Always ask for their business card so they will do the same for you. Good salespeople ask questions and listen. If you are selling business-to-business then professional meetings will become more relevant. Yet, the methods of personal networking within the organization would not vary.

Previous customers should be a significant part of any marketing plan. The definition of previous customers must include those from your present position and those you have served previously—even within other industries. In other words, do not assume that selling stocks will not be relevant to your previous customers in the auto business.

Every industry has a different buying cycle. One may purchase cars every three years and stocks every few months. These buying cycles will determine how often you market and how you market to your customer base. Remember that you are not marketing just for their business but also for referrals.

There is no category that illustrates our adversity for cold calling more than *previous customers*. Why cold call when you have not effectively marketed those you have utilized your most precious resources to serve over the years?

Previous Prospects. Just as you have devoted time and money cultivating relationships with previous customers, those who you DID NOT sell last time around represent a significant investment of your precious resources. Time and money were expended making the phone ring and moving through the sales process. Knowledge was imparted and some level of service delivered. There may even be a measure of guilt because they used your resources and either did not purchase or purchased from someone else. Stephen Covey would say that you have built-up an *emotional bank account*.

Most salespeople ignore previous contacts, perhaps because they have expended resources and have failed to make a sale. Perhaps they do not want to send "good resources after bad." This is a huge mistake in strategy.

Because you have built-up rapport, previous prospects are fertile ground for referrals. What better time to invoke the law of reciprocity—after they have used your services but you have received no value in return.

Times change and so do situations. If previous prospects could not purchase because they were not "qualified," this does not mean that they will not be qualified for the rest of their life. The fact that they have expressed an interest and desire is the most important element. Have you put them in a situation where they will be in a better position to qualify some time in the future? If you have, then you are continuing to impart value to your prospects.

The formula for previous prospects is not much different than for previous customers. Continue to deliver value and this will give you the right to continue to ask for referrals and put you in a position to succeed if and when they are ready to purchase. The time you spend cold calling prevents you from fostering these long-term relationships.

Co-workers. It may seem that the co-worker category will not be helpful to you in prospecting if you are working with other salespeople. After all, wouldn't they be taking advantage of all the prospects themselves? Possibly, but there are a few important points to bear in mind:

♦ Not all salespeople can handle all situations. If you have a particular area of expertise, you may receive referrals from those who do not service this niche—if you prospect within the organization. If your sales organization has offices in other locations, fostering long-distance relationships can be beneficial especially with regard to relocations and long-distance purchases.

♦ Every organization has operational components. Get to know those who make up the operational staff of the company. Take them out to lunch and ask for referrals. The company may pay them for bringing in leads—but it does not mean that you cannot be the recipient of this value.

♦ Reach back into your past. Those who worked with you at previous jobs also represent a major source of referrals. If your previous job was in the same line of sales, there are most likely those who have left the business (also true for your present office) and have previous customers they refer. If your previous job was in another field, these relationships are still more fertile than a cold call. Why not call someone you worked with for five years rather than someone you have never met? Do not worry about not having kept the relationship going. Do not let call reluctance keep you from mining gold.

Professionals. The professional category within our personal sphere of influence is a bit broad and is generally comprised of the professionals within our lives—doctors, lawyers, CPA's, financial planners, etc. There are several reasons why professionals can represent a very lucrative aspect of our marketing plan, such as:

◆ Professionals themselves can represent an important target for many within sales. They earn more money than most any other target group. If one would like to earn more, then sell to those who are in the higher-income brackets.

◆ Professionals (unless they work for corporations or the government) directly serve the public. Therefore, they have great access to potential customers and if you have the ability to grant them access to your customer base a reciprocal relationship can be very beneficial. Imagine a joint mailing from a CPA and a real estate professional or mortgage broker to their respective customer lists. The real estate list would be fertile ground before tax season or after the purchase of their first home. The accountant's list would be fertile ground after the checks to the IRS have just been mailed. Maximum synergy marketing at its best!

◆ Professionals know other professionals. Obviously, if you are an accountant, you will know many other accountants. Your close relationship with a particular professional can lead to relationships with many more. If your target market is accountants (perhaps you are selling office systems), this is the best place to start for referrals.

It is important to note that many segments of your sphere of influence will be related to others. Just as your customer list may be of interest to a professional, your previous customers can also lead you to professionals. If you are helping someone purchase investments, why not ask the advice of their accountant and get them involved?

Vendors. Those pesky salespeople you have been avoiding may be one of your best sources of gold. Of course, you are not a pesky salesperson, you are a professional. It is all the other salespeople in your life . . .

We can divide vendors into two basic categories:

◆ Those who call upon you. Instead of brushing off salespeople, use the fact that they can be especially willing to please you in any way they can (within reason of course). This is especially true regarding those from whom you regularly make purchases. Remember each of these vendors is in the business of knowing many business people and networking is a vital part of their job. *Hmm—people who want to please you and have many contacts . . .*

♦ Vendors who call upon your targets. We are not talking about your competitors here. There is someone calling upon your targets and selling a non-competing product. One day you call upon your target and the next day they call upon your target. Setting up synergy partnerships with these people can be very lucrative because you can double your reach without devoting twice as much time and money. Which is more efficient: a cold call to a prospective target or a call to someone who could help you reach 100 prospects—prospects with whom they already have a relationship?

Hopefully we have made our point. If you cannot find enough calls to make within the many categories we have looked within—from previous customers to vendors—go ahead and cold call. On the other hand, if you really move deeper into your sphere of influence you will find so many choices that cold calling should never become an option. Used correctly, networking is an unbelievably effective synergy marketing tool!

Effective targets with which you have a close relationship or complete strangers. When you look at the choice this way it is no wonder we have also named this section—*Cold Calling (IS) For Dummies.*

Synergy through newsletters

It is not unusual for a sales professional or company to start marketing using a newsletter to keep in touch with their customer base and even more importantly to increase production. As technology becomes more and more commonplace, direct consumer contact will be even more important and there is no customer base that is more important than your *previous customers.* In this regard the definition of previous customer would be broader than your customers—it would also include those who referred customers to you and other vendors involved in the process.

For every business person who succeeds with a great newsletter marketing program, there are four who fail. The concept seems so simple and yet why is it so hard? Perhaps if they didn't violate these basic rules of newsletter marketing:

♦ *Above all, make it consistent.* Inconsistency is the major reason newsletters fail—especially those that are self-published. If you become overwhelmed, are you going to take care of a transaction or write the newsletter? The choice is clear. Even the process of using a *made to order* newsletter can be time consuming if it involves mastheads, printing, labels, stuffing envelopes and more. No marketing technique works without consistency and newsletters are no exception to this rule.

◆ *Make it valuable.* Too many newsletters contain recipes and handy hints for getting stains out of clothing. Do not insult your targets—they can get *House & Home* for $25 yearly. Your customers are interested in more productivity with less stress. So are the businesses that are vendors associated with your customers. Your newsletters should contain hard news and tips to increase income and productivity and make their lives easier.

◆ *Expand your focus.* When you create or purchase a newsletter you now have an asset. Why not utilize maximum synergy rule number five—every action can be made more effective through additional doses of synergy? Offer to send your newsletter to your synergy partner's mailing list and make your database available to your synergy partner in a reciprocal relationship. This can double your reach instantly.

◆ *Make the phone ring.* Your newsletter should have a response mechanism. Why distribute a newsletter that does not make the phone ring? The response mechanism will be more effective than a letter that says, *I make my living off of referrals, so . . .* It should entice the reader to call because the reader will benefit.

◆ *Offer something of value.* The response mechanism must contain something of value. For example, I once followed an article on telephone sales with an offer for sales personnel to receive questions to ask rate shoppers over the phone. More than 300 phone calls were received from this offer. What can you provide of value that will make the phone ring? Value implies more than a coupon for $100 off on their next transaction. This is obviously self-serving. It must be something which is of value to all your readers, whether they are presently purchasing or not.

◆ *Follow-up.* Newsletters can be consistent but they cannot be persistent. Only you can be persistent. All the mailings in the world will not work unless you speak to people constantly. This means following up when the phone rings. It also means asking for referrals when the phone rings. Of course, when you ask for a referral it is absolutely more effective when you have offered something of value that invokes the law of reciprocity. Isn't *do you know anyone else who could benefit from this kind of* _____ more effective than, *I make my living from referrals?*

Another way of following up would be to present dynamic presentations in meetings and/or seminars based upon your newsletter content. As a matter of fact, this is a basic test of newsletter content validity. If the content does not support a dynamic presentation, the content is not valuable.

Once you have mastered these rules of newsletter marketing you will be well on your way to continuing past relationships rather than starting over and over again. Starting new relationships is the greatest waste of your most precious resource—TIME.

News releases—not all marketing is expensive

Marketing costs typically represent the greatest variable expenditure category within a business. Many times we never receive close to the value of our costs with regard to our marketing budget. Usually this is because very little time is spent planning to achieve the greatest effectiveness and more importantly, following up to make sure we achieve this planned effectiveness.

Does this mean that we should stop advertising? Not a likely option for most. It does mean that we should spend our time considering options that will lower our costs and/or increase the effects of our marketing efforts. Is it possible to lower the costs of certain types of marketing to close to zero? Absolutely!

This section addresses just one aspect of low cost marketing—news releases. Many professionals never consider this option because they feel that they do not have anything newsworthy for print. It may be true that sending out a news release regarding what everyone else is doing will achieve little or no response. How can you make what everyone else is doing newsworthy? Try doing something different.

Give a seminar and invite a government specialist to present and broaden the appeal. Now instead of a seminar on estate planning, invite the public to hear an IRS specialist speak about how to survive an audit of your estate moves.

Even the services you advertise can be made newsworthy—especially if you offer a free benefit to the general public. Offer a free article, audio or video regarding preparing a will. Let the general public know by describing the benefit in a news release.

Now that we have the topic, how do we get started? Our first move is to prepare a list (these can be mailing addresses, fax numbers or e-mail addresses) of local media outlets. These should not be hard to find because you probably have been paying to advertise in many of these publications. Your news releases should be directed to the real estate, business or other appropriate editors. Having specific names is even more effective, but keep these names up to date.

Our next step is to write a news release. It is important for news releases to be:

- ◆ succinct—include a number to call to get further information;
- ◆ well written—not to sound like advertising copy; and,
- ◆ timely—not written about an event that will not take place for six months.

We now are ready to *deliver* the piece. With faxes and e-mail, delivery can take place instantaneously—however the good old postal service still works in this regard. Be sure to uncover publication deadlines. Many periodicals that publish weekly or monthly may have submission dates that are weeks or even months in advance.

The final step is to follow-up releases with a phone call. Very few people do this and the increased attention alone might prompt an editor to pay special attention to the story. Remember, they are inundated with mail just as you are. When you call their attention to your story (in a non-obtrusive way) they might very well highlight your story.

Following up also intimates that you will be following up on the story's response. Therefore, it makes sense that all news releases have a response mechanism as should all advertising. If you invite the public to respond in order to receive something for free, you will receive much greater benefit. If a thousand people read your story, it is likely that only a few are ready to take action today. However, those who are thinking about taking an action in the next few years need to be captured and placed in your database for future marketing activities.

More on maximum synergy partnerships

In opening the chapter of this book, we introduce the concept of synergy partnerships. At this juncture, let's delve into this concept more deeply with an additional example. The basic question to ask about your synergy marketing partners: how can they benefit from your marketing efforts and how can you benefit from theirs?

As a matter of fact, the more value you add to the relationship with your synergy partners, the more value you will receive from the relationship. Many believe that providing something of value to a partner actually will cost something of value—namely time or money. Sometimes nothing can be further from the truth. Sometimes your least valuable resource—trash—can be your synergy partner's treasure.

Let us explain. Perhaps a car finance company is advertising utilizing the "Statue of Liberty" technique. This is how such an ad reads:

Give me your poor,
Give me your tired,
Give me your hungry.
(Translation: You breathe—you can purchase a car.)

The same company then complains that they have to wade through piles and piles of leads to get one deal to work. Help! Well, you receive what you advertise. You advertise for junk—you will get junk.

Many of these deals will not close anytime soon. *So, what do you do with the junk you can't work with?* Some place these names within a database so that they can direct mail or call again a year later. Most do nothing—they just throw the names out because they are too busy to set up a long-term plan.

What we have is a multitude of consumers who would like to purchase a car. We can't handle these people because of mountains of debt, poor credit, job histories or often all of the above. This is our garbage. We then send these people away and say, *get your act straightened out and come back in a year.* What are the chances of that happening? They did not get it right over the past 30 years, so what are the chances they are going to straighten their lives out over the next 12 months?

For at least one synergy marketing partner, our garbage is their treasure. What about referring each of these castoffs to a consumer credit counseling service? This would ensure the following:

◆ Instead of sending these people away, we are providing value in terms of the referral of professional assistance.
◆ You will save time. Stop trying to be amateur counselors and call in a professional.
◆ You are increasing the probability that your database will be worthwhile in one year. With professional help, these consumers

are much more likely to achieve their goal of purchasing. Without professional help they are much more likely to wander aimlessly. These consumers already have the most important attribute—desire.

◆ You are providing something of value to someone else. Those who are professional credit counselors may have to advertise to reach the people you have already reached. Now you can save them the money and time.

Of course, the credit counseling service must provide something of value to you. When one of their clients exits counseling, to whom is the service going to refer them when they are able to purchase? The answer is clear—someone who has given value to the consumer and the counseling service.

In other words, the credit counseling service makes a perfect synergy marketing partner. The wider you open your arms during your marketing efforts, the more likely you are going to be wading through your own trash and sifting through someone else's treasure. Why not get paid back for the most important resources you are utilizing—money and time?

As your eyes open wider, you will find that anyone who is operating their marketing plan within a vacuum is not taking advantage of many synergy opportunities that revolve directly outside of their narrow field of vision. Why market alone when you can have many marketing for you? This is what synergy is all about.

Previous customers—where to start the synergy process

Have you ever received a referral, successfully guided a transaction to settlement and then never received another referral from that customer? Perhaps you felt that you had delivered great customer service, followed-up with a thank you note and placed a few perfunctory phone calls. This left you more confused than ever when these same people purchased again sometime in the future but did not purchase from you.

As a sales or business person, time is surely your most precious resource. There is no doubt that within every transaction there is a significant amount of this resource expended. When you have completed a sale, you are likely to have:

◆ made a contact;
◆ developed a rapport;

◆ provided a service; and,

◆ followed-up to make sure everyone involved was satisfied.

The fact that you had to start over again with another customer is a significant waste of time. Every time you start again, you must expend significant amounts of time making contacts and developing rapport. The quality level of referrals will remain low because there is no higher quality of referral than those that come from repeat business.

How can you avoid losing this opportunity time and time again? In order to fully understand how to construct a solution, we must first analyze the reasons that you may have failed to achieve long-term success regarding repeat business. The possibilities exist within three general categories:

1. The first possibility is that you simply did not ask for another referral. As they say when advertising the lottery: *you can't win if you don't play*. Every salesperson knows they could increase their level of production if they just asked more often. It is obvious that we should ask for new sources of business. When we deliver a reasonable level of service to a customer we tend to assume that they would look no place else for their next transaction. The assumption is false. The customer may be swayed by the next person trying to develop a rapport in order to get their business. In other words: even if you were keeping in touch, you did not ask at the right time.

2. The second possibility is that the customer was not as happy with the service as you thought. It could be something you said during the transaction, or perhaps you did not return phone calls as quickly as they would have liked. Did you use a customer service survey?

3. Finally, if there are any questions at all regarding your level of service you definitely did not exceed your customer's expectations. Exceeding expectations is the true definition of excellent customer service. Perhaps you did close the transaction smoothly. In what way did you exceed your target's expectations?

It is clear that your previous customers are a quality source of business—a concept we have discussed in several sections of this book. It is also clear that you must exceed their expectations and take specific actions in order to earn their business again and again and even more importantly, keep those referrals coming.

Public speaking—the maximum synergy tool

Polls have been taken to measure the greatest fears of Americans today. The answer confounds experts. The top fear is not the dentist chair, heights or even death. It is public speaking. What is it about speaking before more than one person that strikes fears in the hearts of the average American today? Do we fear that our tongue will fall out and we will never be able to use it again? Will we turn into a babbling idiot and start drooling on our clothes?

More importantly, if we are so afraid of speaking in public, why do so many strive to become better and more confident public speakers? The bookstores and seminars are full of ideas to help you improve your skills. Why is the attainment of this skill so attractive?

Public speaking is important because it is one of the most effective marketing tools—and our synergy rules dictate that we utilize the most effective tools. We can't think of any other marketing instrument that can match its power.

- While automated marketing systems cost you thousands of dollars—speaking is free.
- Speaking lets you personally reach tens or hundreds of potential customers with your message—in a very short period of time.
- People cannot throw out speeches like junk mail—if they are there and you are good, they will listen.
- People who attend a speech or seminar are generally present because of their own choosing—in other words, they are very qualified candidates.
- You have a chance to instill great confidence regarding your abilities to many people at once.

Direct mail and other automated marketing techniques can be very effective if you deliver the right message to the right person. No method of advertising can be as effective as a direct emotional pitch in person. Selling is a people business and your success is determined by your ability to develop relationships. The problem is that it would take many, many years to develop all the relationships you need one-on-one. There just are so many days in which you can have lunches with potential clients.

Public speaking enables you to make the emotional connection to more than one person at a time. Sure you must follow-up on an individual basis. But given your ability to deliver a coherent message personally to these people, the basis for your starting this relationship will be greatly enhanced. Also, when you turn to these individual relationships, your new skill will enable you to speak one-on-one with more confidence.

Let's say that you deliver a seminar on retirement planning to an audience of 20. First, we can assume that each attended because they are interested in preparing for retirement or some time in the future. Now you have qualified candidates. If five of these attendees approach you directly after the seminar to ask questions, you have started the second stage of the bonding process with a handful of people. Now you know that a certain number of people have a higher level of interest and may be more immediate prospects. How many cold calls over the telephone and follow-up meetings would it take to reach this stage while prospecting?

If you are a great public speaker you will be able to deliver a message that will attract people to you. Direct mail pieces work very hard at establishing creditability: *read me—I am good—a number one producer*. Anything to get the phone to ring. Seeing you perform and conquer in public reaches people in a way that no advertising piece can ever match.

Finally, public speaking is such a great tool because not many people do it well or effectively. Attend any marketing seminar and they will tell you to market by making yourself look different. People then spend thousands of dollars concocting major schemes to shoot themselves from cannons in public—*Look at me, I am different*. In reality, it only takes something everyone already has to look different—your mouth. You should do it and do it well because your competitors can't.

Of course, what good are all of these benefits if an individual cannot bear to utter more than one word to a group of two individuals without turning to jelly? Many would love to use the power of public speaking but don't see any way of making it happen. They might as well be standing on one side of the grand canyon with a pot of gold on the other side.

Fortunately, for those who are highly motivated, the fear of public speaking can be conquered. We just need to recognize that overcoming our fear of public speaking will take hard work, determination and patience. All worthy goals are achieved one step at a time. You cannot expect to go away for a week and come back from a program as an accomplished speaker. There are some excellent books (as well as organizations, such as Toastmasters and the National Speakers Association) such as *WAKE'EM UP* by Tom Antion (Anchor Publishing, 1997) and *Speak and Grow Rich* by Dottie and Lilly Walters (Prentice Hall, 1989) that can help you attain the goal of competent public speakers.

What is the key to achieving great public speaking abilities? The Four P's:

Practice

Preparation

Performance

Persistence

Practice. There is no factor which is more important than practice. No baseball player makes it to the major leagues without practice. No salesperson becomes a top producer without practice.

It is practice that leads us to make progress one step at a time. If you had to appear before 300 people but your only task was to utter the word *"you,"* the situation would not seem as ominous. Well, start by practicing small segments of a talk: just a few sentences. Use something with which you are very familiar—for example if you are selling cars, relate your first car buying experience as a teenager. Perhaps you were totally scared over a payment that was 80 dollars per month 20 years ago.

Practice these sentences by yourself, over and over. Practice in front of a mirror so that you can practice your speaking gestures as well. Perhaps you are biting your lip as you speak. Tape yourself so that you can hear your voice. Many times we cannot hear ourselves inserting a *you know* after every sentence because it represents an ingrained habit.

After you have practiced these few sentences hundreds of times, start practicing in front of those you know—your pets, your family and your friends. Then move up to a tougher audience—your peers in a sales meeting. Perhaps you could get together with several other salespeople and perform together. This is the concept of Toastmasters: a group of people helping each other better their public speaking abilities. Toastmaster meetings are a great place to learn and practice (for information on a club in your area, visit www.toastmasters.org).

Preparation. Practice makes you more comfortable with the material because you know it so well. Preparation makes you comfortable with the engagement because it puts you in command of the situation.

We suggest your first official speaking engagement be for only a few people. If you are already a salesperson, you should be comfortable giving a sales pitch one-on-one. The next step is to deliver this pitch to a few people. How can you prepare?

◆ Speak to the participants ahead of time. Familiarize yourself with their backgrounds and their expectations. Later on when you speak to larger groups, you can interview one or two leading members of the audience and customize your remarks to match their needs. This will enable you to improve your general substance through tailoring and obtain other details such as the proper dress.

◆ Arrive at the event at least one hour ahead of time. Look over the lighting, seating arrangements and acoustics. Fix anything that needs to be fixed now, before the group arrives.

◆ Use handouts, slides, overhead transparencies, and/or notes. Being prepared with your visual aids will ensure that you will not lose your place. Do not read from your notes—this is what practice is supposed to eliminate. It is perfectly acceptable to refer to your notes periodically. Handouts or slides with bulleted points serve as great visual effects for participants and as a guide for you.

The proper preparation is no less important if you are talking to three people or a hundred. All the practice in the world will not help unless you are prepared for anything that can happen. When you are prepared for a disaster you no longer will fear that calamity. You are now ready to perform!

Perform. We have spent the last few days, weeks and months practicing, practicing and practicing. It is now time to put on the show. Where do we go? Try . . .

◆ Large employers, who might let you hold an informal gathering in the company cafeteria.

◆ Government agencies with large employment bases.

◆ Civic organizations such as the Chamber of Commerce. Many of the members are financial planners, CPA's and attorneys who could have tremendous networking value for you.

◆ Holding your own seminar in a public library or a local hotel.

The possibilities are endless. Of course, you must decide what to say in front of these groups. A couple of rules to follow when deciding what topic would be appropriate:

◆ First, speak to their interests and not yours. They know that you sell something for a living. If you are speaking to a group of financial planners, then you must explain how your product will help them achieve goals for their clients.

◆ Customize the presentation. Canned presentations do not work before all audiences. Speak to representatives beforehand and find out all information possible. Perhaps a downsizing just occurred. How would you approach your presentation differently with this knowledge in hand?

◆ Generate a goal for each presentation. No presentation will be beneficial to you unless you achieve your own objectives. Do these objectives include walking away with leads in your pocket, scheduling another presentation or the long-term objective of being a resource for the group organizing the meeting?

◆ Organize the presentation. Start with a strongly worded statement regarding why your topic is important. Within the body, back up your statements. End with a summary that includes instructions regarding how they can take action.

◆ Distribute an evaluation at the end of the presentation. The positive comments can be used to capture more presentations and the calls for improvement can help you make adjustments in the future. You might make sure that everyone participates in the evaluation by holding your door prize until the end and selecting from the evaluations.

Persist. You have identified the group and the topic. The big day arrives. Your still nervous? Even with all of your preparation and practice? Do not be alarmed as this is normal. Even the greatest of professionals get tight right before they perform. There are a few tricks that will help you become more comfortable.

First, since you have arrived early to set up, take the time to meet much of your audience in advance. Once you know your audience well, they will be pulling for you and you will be talking to friends.

Second, imagine the worst that can happen. Perhaps the worst thing you can think of would be to completely go blank. What would you do in this case? Perhaps you would begin reading your notes. Once you face the worst from a mental standpoint, reality will not seem as bad. The important thing is to remember that the audience has no idea what you are going to say. Therefore, if you miss a point or two no one will notice or care.

It may seem traditional to start the audience off with a joke (A funny thing happened to me on the way . . .). Instead, try starting off by relating a personal story. You will soon learn that people remember very little of what you say (that is why missing points is not so important). What they will remember will be the stories and the pictures (visuals). The more stories you tell, the more human you will become and the more the audience will relate to you.

Even more important, the more likable and human you become to the audience, the more likely they will want to do business with you in the future. This is why it is important for you not to speak behind a lectern with little or no energy. Make sure you get plenty of rest the day before and get ready to move around. Look at the eyes within your audience and try to relate on their level. Walk around the room and up the aisles, smiling as you go. The more you become part of the audience, the more comfortable you will become. A comfortable public speaker? Watch out, you now have a powerful synergy tool at your disposal.

Referrals—the synergy mindset

We cover the importance of referrals as opposed to cold calling in several places within this book. Therefore, we thought it would be good to present some advice from a referral expert. Bill Cates is the author of the popular book *Unlimited Referrals,* and the creator of *The Unlimited Referrals Marketing Systems*®. He is also a highly sought after speaker. His books and audio tapes can be purchased through Referral Coach International (800-488-5464 or www.ReferralCoach.com). Let's turn it over to Bill . . .

Your foundation to building your business with referrals is the set of attitudes you bring to your prospecting efforts—your referral mindset. In my *Unlimited Referrals Seminar*, I share nine attitudes you must develop and use to create the most powerful action in gaining an unlimited supply of high-quality endorsed referrals.

You have a referral mindset, when . . .

1. You understand that your prospects prefer to meet you through referrals over any other method and it's the most cost effective way to attract new clients.
2. Rather than transactions, you look to the lifetime value of a client—not just the business they can do with you, who they will meet and connect with you over their lifetime.
3. You move beyond rapport and form relationships of real trust.
4. You have an *attitude of service.* You know it's the fastest way to earn someone's trust.

5. You give referrals whenever you can. You are a resource who connects people.

6. You ask for referrals whenever you see the right opportunity. You don't wimp out.

7. You realize that asking for referrals is an extension of the service you bring to the marketplace.

8. You create a pleasant and valuable "experience" around the referral process, from how you ask, to how you contact the prospect, to how you celebrate the process.

9. You expect to get referrals. You expect people to engage in the referral process, your awareness changes, and your actions become more effective.

Bill's work covers many other aspects of the referral process such as methods of gaining a personal introduction, ways to thank your referral sources and alternatives for asking for the referral. Understanding the referral process is an important part of marketing. It is more a science rather than an art. It is important to note that any referral system will not work without the delivery of value and the corresponding build-up of trust within your clients (the last and most important synergy rule). The best time to ask is when your client recognizes the value you've brought to them—but if you don't use a proven process for asking you are less likely to achieve a successful response.

Relationships mean never starting over . . .

We have already established that your previous customer base should always be your most important target. Sales is a relationship business. We spend an inordinate amount of time trying to develop relationships with people we don't know while we ignore those that already exist. With our previous customers we have already expended a tremendous amount of energy:

> We have made a contact . . .
> We have converted a lead . . .
> We have delivered a service . . .

Why start over and over again, making cold calls when you can be building upon these relationships? There is nothing less stressful than repeat business from a previous customer or a personal referral. We start the sales process with an element of trust that has to be earned when dealing with cold leads.

To take advantage of these relationships we cannot assume that referred business will walk in the door. We must nurture these relationships, letting them grow. We can't do this by keeping in touch once every three years. We must be in touch constantly. We can't be in touch using sticky notes. Sticky notes do not constitute an effective follow-up system. Here is what will help us effect great follow-up:

Computerized contact management systems. Yes, to effectively keep in touch you must have a computer with a database and contact management software. The database must have relevant information about your clients (e.g., their purchase date and preferences). The contact management function must record your previous conversations so that you are up to date. Speaking to the customer infrequently, it is hard to remember all of the relevant details of your previous conversation. On the other hand, if you start out with a question such as *"How is that __?"* they know that you cared enough to remember them, which further elevates the level of trust.

The contact management system should also group customers according to categories that will help you target certain segments of your database (see the Networking Section). It should also let you know when important dates are approaching through an alarm system. Each day, your computer should let you know to whom you should be making a follow-up phone call or sending another form of communication.

Providing value. You must provide value to your database on a regular basis. Letters are not valuable (letters may contain offers of value). Newsletters, articles and other information are extremely valuable if they are targeted to your clients' needs. So are offers for other professional services that may enhance the lives of your clients. The delivery of value brings the ultimate synergy.

Third-party value. Sending a communication that offers something of value provided by another party serves two purposes. It diversifies the value that you can offer. It also provides value to that party by providing access to your customers. Of course, you would expect reciprocity. In other words, you can now increase the size of your database to include their contacts.

Response mechanisms. Do not merely send the value. Send an offer to provide the value. This will cause your customers to call to request the item. Every telephone conversation is an opportunity to fill needs for your clients and ask for additional referrals. Calling a thousand customers to determine which one has a need is much more difficult than using a response mechanism so that they selectively call you when they have a need.

Hold an event. Special events for your personal clients are a great way to follow with several at once. Perhaps it could be a seminar with a synergy partner. Remember, this event is not merely to sell but to provide value. Allow them to invite a guest. Other options include hosting a reception or renting a theatre for a showing of a first-run movie.

Keeping in touch is just the first step. The key is providing value to your customers on a regular basis so that your relationships are continually upgraded. It sure beats cold calls.

Seminars for synergy

As we perfect our public speaking skills, we are in a position to discover a *made for synergy marketing tool*—seminar presentations. Within several industries, seminars are a frequently utilized marketing device.

- ◆ Financial planners present seminars on retirement planning;
- ◆ Accountants and/or attorneys present seminars on estate planning;
- ◆ Realtors® and/or mortgage companies present seminars for first time homebuyers; and,
- ◆ Web design companies present seminars on web design and marketing.

Seminars may be presented by the business or through a sponsoring trade association. It would not be unusual for an annual conference of an association to contain one or more seminars presented by vendors of the industry. Many vendors are active within their target associations (they may be called affiliate members) for the primary purpose of achieving such exposure.

Why are seminars so conducive to the utilization of our maximum synergy rules? The connection is quite obvious:

- ◆ Seminars enable us to utilize one of our most effective tools— public speaking. Speaking publicly enables us to establish instant credibility as we reach a large segment of our targets simultaneously.
- ◆ Seminars are a perfect forum for the involvement of our synergy partners. If we are presenting a seminar, it costs us nothing to have it sponsored by a partner. In fact, the sponsor may help us defray the cost of the seminar and can help us with the marketing efforts. Why reach one target audience when we can reach a second for

free? In this respect, it is important to attempt to include a government agency or association as a "free sponsor." This adds even more credibility to the event and may enable you to reach a larger audience. It also adds extra value to an entity that may be able to deliver much in return.

◆ Seminars enable us to deliver value to our most effective target. We should be reaching out to our previous customers with our seminars as well as prospects. This will dictate that our seminar topics be broadened to include value to another segment of our target audience. In the case of a real estate agent, a first time home-buyer seminar would not be appropriate for previous customers. A seminar on using a home to leverage investments or to move in position to purchase a move-up home would be appropriate. Our previous customers are valuable because they may purchase again and are an important source of referrals. If we don't deliver value to them, we will not be in a position to be asking for referrals.

◆ Seminars are the perfect opportunity to accomplish two objectives with one action. Potential multiple objectives will include more than those already mentioned through synergy partnerships and present customers. Seminars give you the opportunity to add multiple objectives to your advertising schemes. All too often we cannot market for our seminars effectively because it is "in addition" to our other marketing efforts. In reality, seminar marketing should be integrated into all present marketing activities, including newsletters to your sphere of influence, direct mail, newspaper ads, the Internet and more. There is no reason not to add an invitation to the seminar to all present advertising copy.

◆ The seminar itself is an excellent opportunity to build your long-term database. All too often we target hot prospects at the seminar and ignore those who do not respond immediately. Marketing and sales are long-term processes and if we do not keep in touch with the majority of attendees we are wasting the resources we have utilized in advertising and delivering this value.

Seminars represent an excellent opportunity to differentiate yourself from your competitors. You are much more likely to be recognized as delivering value if you are undertaking an activity that is unique. If your competitors are not using this marketing vehicle, you are in a great position to stand out from the crowd. If they are using this marketing vehicle, you have an opportunity to differentiate yourself by presenting a new topic. Actually, the material does not have to be as different as the title itself—

"Buying your first home" might be advertised as

"Purchasing a home using someone else's money"
"Protecting your assets from the IRS" might be advertised as
"Make sure the IRS does not make your children start over"

Finally, do not forget the most important sales trait without which you can render the most effective marketing tool useless. You can market your seminar effectively, attract a great crowd and deliver significant value, but if you do not ask for business you will never receive a return on your investment. Too many give great seminars and assume the value will translate into business. This assumption is false. It is important to "work" asking into the content of the seminar rather than making a plea for business at the end.

For instance, you might take an example from the audience instead of presenting your own fictitious case. These examples will alert you to business opportunities within the audience. Using an evaluation at the end of the seminar will not only garner important feedback, but it is also an opportunity to ask for specific referrals (see the section on customer service surveys within the Customer Service Chapter).

Telemarketing

Literally, telemarketing denotes the use of the telephone for the purpose of marketing. In reality, the marketing is often accomplished before the phone call is placed and the call is utilized to close the sale—hence the term *telesales*. The process of telemarketing or telesales can follow a few different formulas.

- ◆ Automatic or manual dialing of *cold* prospects. The automated feature may be in conjunction with live telesales operators (predictive dialers) or an automated message delivery system (the automated system's objectives would be to produce warm leads).
- ◆ Dialing of warm leads. These leads may have been produced through a marketing campaign, for example registration on an Internet site, visitors to a trade show exhibit or leads produced through an automated message delivery.
- ◆ In-bound receipt of warm leads. Warm leads may be responding to a marketing campaign (mass media or direct mail) advertising an 800 number.

Professional telemarketing operations will verify that warm leads present much higher closing rates than cold calling (which our previous discussions have already emphasized). Anytime someone is responding to a solicitation there is an expression of need. In the absence of warm leads, the process of market research is very important with regard to the determination of the specific target audience. Cold calling is characterized by conversion rates that are so low, a target audience that is off by the smallest amount can cause the campaign to be extremely cost prohibitive.

Professional telemarketing systems are available through outsourcing. The technology of autodialers and CRM (customer relationship management) software analysis systems are so sophisticated that it may become cost-prohibitive for smaller companies to effectively telemarket in-house. Sophisticated operations can select the appropriate data for solicitation, script the sales pitch, track all levels of responses and systematically test several aspects of the sale, including:

◆ pricing schemes;
◆ conversion rates for different demographic groups;
◆ variation in sales scripts; and,
◆ optimum calling conditions (timing, voice mail messages, etc.).

Telemarketing can be utilized for direct consumer operations (home equity lines, mortgages) or business-to-business sales (professional publications, memberships). In either case, the production of warm leads can increase the effectiveness of the efforts. It is in this case that response mechanisms are imperative. Synergy requires all marketing to contain response mechanisms—especially those that offer value to the majority of recipients. It is this value that increases the response rate and produces a greater proportion of warm leads.

The proper training of telemarketing personnel in the art of synergy can move the operation towards greater productivity in the long run. For example, telemarketers can be trained to ask for referrals even from those who are responding negatively to their pitches—especially if they are offering something of value. Each referral in effect becomes another warm lead and will produce greater results than a cold call.

Trades shows—stirring the synergy pot

My vision of working a trade show goes back to my time as a loan officer in the early 1980s. We had a trade show for Realtors® and I was to join my fellow loan officers "working the booth." I arrived for the second shift, which was three hours after the exhibit hall was open for business.

I walked through the hall and eyed the competition. In many cases, I lingered long enough to grab some literature. Typically, those behind the tables smiled and some even said hello. Few bothered to get up from their chairs. Some just sat back with their hands folded behind their head. When I asked them how the convention was going, they complained that the Realtor® traffic was slow and the attendees were just stuffing their bags with goodies. The prevailing opinion was that this event was a waste of time.

Trade shows utilize the two most precious resources of an organization—time and money. The results achieved must be commensurate with the resources expended. I do believe that if a developed marketing plan is put into place almost all trade shows can deliver a home run in terms of marketing synergy.

Prepare. If you are running around at the last minute trying to find items to give away at the booth and searching for adequate coverage, these are sure signs of the lack of adequate preparation. Your preparation should include:

◆ Reviewing the agenda for the trade show—including seminars, cocktail hours and other events;
◆ Reviewing the potential attendance with the show's sponsors;
◆ Reviewing the other vendors and their placement within the hall;
◆ Determining the best strategic placement for your booth within the hall; and,
◆ Your plan for marketing collateral, technical presentations, promotional items, offers and drawings.

Set your goals. Unless you have specific goals for the program, it is unlikely you will realize whether the event was a success. These goals might include increasing the size of your database, actual sales effected at the event, follow-up sales, meetings set-up afterwards, etc. Your goals should dictate your actions during the program. For example, a promotion may be set which encourages the attendees to take a specific action. If your goal is to create name identification, the promotion may be unrelated to the actual sale. Of course, maximum synergy rule number one indicates that you should be achieving more than one objective at the trade show.

Participate. Maximum effectiveness is achieved by participating in all aspects of the event. If there are seminars, can your company supply a speaker? If not, attend the seminar and participate with questions. If there is a cocktail party, this will represent an opportunity to network in a more intimate atmosphere as opposed to across the table.

Capture names. Many event sponsors will provide the attendee list to exhibitors. In addition, there should be a basket for a drawing on your table. Make the drawing something valuable from a business perspective instead of a basket of fruit (perhaps a PDA or a book on marketing). You might choose to have an "event special" tied to attendees who purchase within ____ days of the event or take a specific action at the event (such as fill in a registration form). Adding a sense of urgency never hurts.

Capture their attention. We are not talking about free massages (though this is an effective technique to attract a crowd). We are talking about personal one-on-one attention. Attracting their attention does not dictate that we tackle a conference attendee as they walk by. It does mean that we are standing upright (perhaps even in front of the table) close enough to make eye contact. Simply ask them how they are doing. With most, eye contact and a simple statement will be enough to get them to stop and give you a small amount of attention. Then follow with another easy question such as *how are you enjoying the show?* This will be a pleasant diversion from those who look like they would like to be somewhere else or still others who are tackling them. Continue the conversation on a personal level with such questions as, *where did you come in from,* and steer it slowly to the business topic as naturally as possible. Five minutes developing a rapport with one person is much more valuable than grabbing ten cards in five minutes.

Find the maximum synergy. Synergy rules dictate that you find the most effective target at an exhibit. The majority of time the most effective target will not be ten prospects, but one or more synergy marketing partners. The hall should be full of potential partners each of whom could lead you to multiple relationships in the future. By reviewing the vendor list ahead of the event you can pinpoint your targeted approach. Perhaps you can set up dinner with two or three non-competing vendors after the hall closes.

Learn about the competition. Trade shows represent excellent venues for learning about the competition. You should witness several of them in attendance and many will be just as curious about your company as you are about theirs. Spend some time at their booths and pick up as much material as possible. While you are there, listen to their presentations to other visitors. Be as open as possible in the sharing of general information. You are not likely to learn unless you share.

Be unique. You can appear unique in your attendance at the trade show (by selecting an event where the competition is not), through your actions at the show (perhaps through a particular promotion) or by providing value (seminar or articles). If you are one of 20 competitors all with product information and baskets of fruit, how are you going to appear different? The answer to this question is the key to achieving maximum synergy. Not feeling innovative? Try *Off-The-Wall Marketing Ideas* by Michaels and Karpowicz (Adams Media Corporation, 2000).

Follow-up. One sentence will suffice—*if you don't follow-up, all the resources expended at the trade show will be rendered worthless.*

Value niche—ultimately synergy must lead here

Most salespeople have a hard time finding their value niche—a niche that differentiates them and makes them unique from their competition.

This is why most advertising focuses upon price or speed. *"Save $$$$"* or *"Sell It Faster."* Sometimes we think that our advertising strategies should be based upon the marketing campaigns of pizza franchises.

Why is it so hard to discover our value niche? For one thing, the value must be matched to the needs of our targets. Many have not even focused enough to define their target base. If we haven't specified our target, it is unlikely we can deliver value that will be right on the money.

What is your target? Is it a particular geographic area? Upscale demographics? A particular transition population such as the recently separated or divorced? When you differentiate each of these targets from the general populace it is easy to see how their needs may differ from one to the next.

Defining our target is not enough. It just gives us the basis for zeroing in upon the needs of our customers. You might assume that you know what is needed by a particular group. But if the need is so obvious, you are guaranteed to be delivering the same value as your competition. Obvious solutions are obvious to everyone playing in the ball game.

A basic rule of marketing value is to make sure that your value is unique. This is why we sometimes refer to this as your value niche. It is easy to see that it can't be a niche if everyone else is occupying the same space. Ask yourself, is your marketing focus and value delivery unique?

So how do we become unique? For one thing, we accomplish market research. We ask our prospects and previous customers questions. We discover their objectives and then uncover the barriers which frustrate them as they attempt to achieve their objectives. We open our eyes wider in order to find opportunities that will actually achieve results beyond their original objectives.

We should also spend some time looking within ourselves. What skill do you have that would make you different from your competition? Whether you are an excellent golfer or a top-notch public speaker, you may have a skill that your target group desires.

We tend to use the term *value-added*, but we sometimes don't really understand the term. The term means that we go beyond the aspirations of those we are striving to serve—beyond their needs and the service of competitors and into a zone reserved for our own niche.

Years ago when my company developed plans for a value-added newsletter, we spent much time researching the scope of the competition and interviewing those we would propose to serve. It was then we decided not to deliver recipes and handy homeowner hints. We needed to deliver value that would help business people sell more with less stress and, in addition, enable their customers—homeowners—to make their ownership experience more profitable as they integrate this ownership into their long-term financial plans.

So what can you deliver? Let's take an example. Suppose your clientele is upscale. What if you are selling investments to those within upper income brackets? Their investment must be part of their long-term economic plan. This translates into more than proposing a wealth building strategy. It takes into account strategies for taxes, retirement and inheritance. How liquid will the investment be? How far are they from retirement? How can your product meet more than one of their needs?

Not all niches are as easy to identify. However, if you are interested in being more successful in the future, the time spent developing a value package will be well worth the effort.

Uniqueness solves the value puzzle

Are you currently achieving your goals?

If you are achieving all of your goals, you might want to skip this section. If not, let's ask a second very important question.

*Are you serious about achieving the goals
you are not currently reaching?*

If the answer to the second question is yes, we are going to ask you to do just one thing . . .

Be different.

We are not asking you to be the most unique person in the world. We are challenging you to do something that . . .

You never have done before . . .
You used to do, but don't do any more (back to basics) . . .
Will be more effective than what you are currently doing.

Sound too simple? We have said several times that the true definition of insanity is doing something again and again and expecting a different result. In other words, if you are going to change your results, you must change your current actions. Don't keep waiting and waiting as you become comfortable. Don't become part of the furniture to those around you.

How different are we talking about? Well, we are not asking you to visit your targets in your underwear! We are asking that you change any activity that is not achieving the results you would like to achieve.

- ◆ If you are mailing—change your mailing piece, change your target, or change your message. Perhaps you can integrate a value-added offer as a response mechanism.
- ◆ If you are telemarketing—change the script, change the target or vary the hours.
- ◆ If you are holding events—do it on a weekend no one normally works (such as July 4th), advertise it in a different way, hold a contest for all visitors, or have a vendor/partner follow-up with a call to the visitors.

There is absolutely nothing you are doing that should be held back from change—unless the activity is achieving the results you would like. If your mailing pieces garner the amount of business you would like, don't change the content. But if your overall business is too slow, then mail with a different message or more often!

The message here is more than just change, it is change to do something that everyone else is not doing. The secret of success is being different. This means different from your competition. You can see what successful companies have brought to America:

Who brought pizza in thirty minutes or less?
Who delivered when you absolutely, positively needed it overnight?
Who eliminated medicine breath?

The reason you know these companies without their names is because they were unique when they delivered their initial message. Now they have competition, because others will copy successful companies. However, this was not before these messages helped them achieve leadership positions within their industries.

So what do you do that is unique? Is your message unique? Is your service unique? Is the way you deliver it unique? Can you describe it in one sentence or less within your voice mail message? If not, it is time for a change. If you have not discovered or cannot describe your Unique Selling Proposition (USP), you will never move away from the pack. Maximum synergy is achieved by delivering value. Something you are delivering is less likely to be valuable if it is not unique.

The Hershman Group? We bring *more productivity with less stress* to small businesses, salespeople and managers across the nation.

Voice mail—use the tool or get lost

Inbound Voice Mail. Technology . . . Some of us are scared of technology. Others embrace it with open arms and make it a full partner in our arsenal. Still others take the plunge only to be lost forever. While many of your competitors are *surfing the net* and discovering innovative ways to reach their targets, others are still trying to figure out how to work that dang telephone system.

While giving major training sessions on customer service skills for sales and operations personnel, I often pose the question: *how many of you can work the call forwarding and conference call features within your telephone systems?* The truth is that less than half of corporate America are comfortable with these features—yet they are essential to execute basic customer service functions such as the smooth transfer of customers between departments.

The same can be said for our voice mail systems. While some of us are using voice mail as major sales instruments, others are still trying to learn how to change their messages. Ann Landers in her column once focused upon those who left messages on the wrong answering machines. *"If those people had left their name and numbers, instead of saying 'call me back because I want to break the engagement,' then I would have been able to let them know that they reached the wrong machine,"* wrote perplexed.

If those answering machines contained recordings that easily identified the occupants of the residence, those who were calling would never have left these messages. This is not rocket science. The secret to great sales and customer service is great communication. The secret of great communication is being clear, concise and specific. Your voice mail message may be the first contact you will have with a prospect. How effective is: *"Leave a message after the beep,"* or *"I am not at my desk right now."* Is this the first communication you would like a prospect to hear from you?

Our message is our chance to communicate. Many security experts advise homeowners to say, *"I am away from the phone right now,"* rather than, *"We are away from home,"* so that would-be burglars are not tipped off. Do you really think that the burglars are that dumb to think that you change your message each time you leave the house? Likewise, do you think that whoever is calling you at the office doesn't know that you are either away from your desk or on the phone when you don't answer? Why state the obvious as your message?

What are the alternatives? There are plenty. If you are going to be unreachable for a certain number of hours, let the callers know when you will be able to get back to them. The second secret to great sales and customer service is great follow-up. If they leave a message and they don't get a call back in three or four hours, is it because of poor follow-up skills? Without a message to the contrary, they will think the worst.

One of the greatest abilities of voice mail systems is to direct people who may be calling the wrong entity or need very simple information. If you call a business today, you can receive directions by pushing the right button. So why not give commonly sought information as a part of the message or with a push-button alternative? Be careful of too many push button alternatives. Don't expect callers to wade through push 1 if you speak English . . . 18 if you wear size 9 shoes. In these situations technology does not help, it hinders the facilitation of communication.

Finally, if you have a *Unique Selling Proposition (USP),* why not let everyone know by making it a part of your message? For example, if a guarantee is part of your sales and customer service regimen, let everyone know who calls. Keep the message short or give an option to leave a communication without listening to the whole ball of wax. If you don't have something unique to sell in one sentence or less, then you have uncovered a great need for your sales arsenal. Sometimes the greatest lesson we learn comes from what we cannot put on our voice mail message. If you just can't think of anything to say except, *"I am not at my desk, leave a message at the beep,"* you just might have to rethink the whole sales process.

Outbound Voice Mail. There is no way around it. If we are going to communicate, we are going to be leaving voice mail messages for our clients. Just you and a hundred other people leaving a voice mail and expecting the call to be returned. Just how do you break through? Here are a few tips you might find helpful:

♦ As Harvey Mackay, author of *Swim With The Sharks* says: *know the gatekeeper.* When calling a business, it is usually extremely helpful to know the person who puts you into voice mail. You have heard it a thousand times before: would you like me to take a message or would you like to go into voice mail? What do you know about the person who is talking? Could this person direct you regarding the best way to communicate a message? Perhaps the gatekeeper could personally deliver a message. Perhaps they could retrieve the answer and communicate back to you. Of course, this will only happen if you develop a relationship.

♦ *Night diversions.* If the gatekeeper's system is so strong that they will not even send you into voice mail, you may have to call directly into automated systems in the off hours in order to reach the personal voice mail of a prospect. Sometimes gatekeepers are instructed to keep solicitations out of the voice mail system. In this case personal messages may only be reaching the round file.

♦ *Ask your customer.* If they want you to keep in touch, they will let you know the best way to reach them. But only if you ask. Many will say: *If you get my voice mail, dial 0 and have the receptionist find me.* Others may give you the best times to get through. You will never know unless you ask.

♦ *Not more than two messages.* True, the first could have been lost. After two, you will be considered a pest. If you really need to get through to this person—reach someone live and find out if they are in the office. Hold a reasonable amount of time until they are available. If they are out of the office—call again without leaving a message: *I'm on the road—I'll just call back.*

♦ *When you do leave a message, make sure it is coherent.* Some people have no idea what their message sounds like on tape. Pronounce your name slowly and if you are not a known entity, spell the name. Most importantly, say your phone number slowly and repeat it twice. If one digit comes out unrecognizable, there is no message. Do not assume that they have your number—even if they know you well. They may be retrieving messages from a place where your number is not accessible. It is rude not to leave a number and to leave a message when you know that they will get a voice mail in return. Let them know when the best time is to return the call and reach you. You might go as far as to set up a tentative telephone appointment. They can leave a message on your voice mail if the time slot you left is not convenient. If you are calling from a cell, the basic rule is that if you cannot hear their voice mail message clearly, the message you leave will not be clear to them. In this case, call back with a clearer connection before going into their voice mail.

◆ *Don't sell by voice mail.* The message should be short. If you give your sales presentation over the phone, they are more likely not to call you back. Simply state: *John Estes ask me to contact you.* This is why networking is so important. If John Estes is a close contact, they will call you back. For all they know, you are a potential customer for them.

When you do leave a message, what do you say? One advantage of voice mail is that you can take care of business through a specific message. *If you will send me this document . . .* There is no doubt that voice mail is an advantage in this regard. We have already indicated that leaving too specific of a message can give the target a reason not to call you back. *I was calling to see if you are interested in some investment opportunities . . .* If the person is not interested, or is not ready to make a decision, they may not return the phone call.

Some targets get angry when you leave a message that doesn't include the purpose of the call—*If you had told me that you were calling about life insurance I wouldn't have called back!* Are you interested in making everyone happy or obtaining more business? It is not rude to leave a clear message with the information needed to reach you but without all the details of the purpose of the call.

Want to leave a substantive message and still get the call returned? Try leaving a message that is unique—whether it be off-beat, funny or interesting. Mark Victor Hansen (co-author of the *Chicken Soup For The Soul* series) reports leaving a simple message: *It is good news.* He says that his messages are returned first because all the other messages are usually no news or bad news. Perhaps you could leave an interesting fact about the prospect's industry. What message could you leave that is unique and would pique their interest enough that they would not only return your call, but return it first?

The best way to ensure that you can have such a message is to ensure you are calling for a reason. If you are calling to touch base or to see if they have made a decision, there is not much to leave by way of a message. If you have something of value to relay or offer, the development of a unique message is much easier.

CHAPTER SIX
Maximum Synergy Management

"The entire sum of existence is the magic of being needed by just one person"
Vi Putnam

It has been almost 15 years since I wrote my text for the mortgage industry—*Managing a Branch Office* (Mortgage Bankers Association, 1987). In this text, I delve into the complexity of management—from profit and loss statements to setting up a retail office. After more than 20 years and thousands of personnel managed, I find that the complexities of management are really quite simple. The rules are as follows:

- ◆ Hire the right people (recruiting, interviewing, reference checking);
- ◆ Agree on the responsibilities of the job (orientation, setting goals);
- ◆ Give them the tools necessary to do the job (coaching, training, marketing support);
- ◆ Get out of the way (communicate); and,
- ◆ Fire your mistakes quickly (you will make them).

It is not any more complex than this. Unfortunately, reality is harder than theory. If hiring the right person was so easy, managing would be a snap. It isn't. We all have our jobs to do—and for many managers this job includes selling and administering. In reality we don't have time to recruit, train and coach the way we should. And when we hire the wrong people and do not coach them well, the job gets even harder.

The answer? The truth of the matter is nothing will make the job of managing people easy. However, several doses of synergy can help our effectiveness and lower our stress levels tremendously. This chapter will not teach you how to manage, it will teach you how to integrate synergy into your management activities and thereby increase your effectiveness. Remember, all improvement comes one step at a time.

And the goal of improved management skills and action is a worthy one. I believe that management is the most rewarding job in the world. We can actually affect the lives and careers of many individuals through our management skills. I know I have touched hundreds of people as I personally have led them and their managers and have trained thousands upon thousands more. When you make a difference in someone's life, you become more than a manager. You become a leader.

Recruiting—the first step

Sales management is one of the most difficult jobs. Many sales managers are personal producers and produce at a level that constituted a full-time job before they became managers. After 50 percent of their time or more is taken by their personal caseload, how much time is left to dedicate to great management skills?

Unfortunately, the majority of the rest of a sales manager's time is quickly absorbed by fighting fires. It is said that 80 percent of a manager's supervisory time is utilized by 20 percent of the poorest performers. This leaves precious time for a manager's most important task—recruitment.

Why is recruitment a manager's most important task? A manager can possess the best management skills in the world, but if that manager hires the wrong people their life is going to be a supervisory nightmare. Rule #1 of great leadership is to hire the right people. Most managers cannot hire the right people because they do not have the time to dedicate to a great recruitment plan. This is because they are spending their time trying to fix the wrong people. Sounds like a vicious cycle? You bet it is!

The question remains: *How do we break out of this vicious cycle?* We could outline a recruitment plan that would absorb ten hours of a manager's time each week. The actions would look great on paper. In reality, there would be no implementation of such a plan. Our sales managers do not have an extra ten hours each week to expend, no matter how much time and stress it will save them in the long run. The only solution is to find synergies between the manager's present activities and our recruitment objectives.

Starting the process . . .

The process must start with the identification of the perfect candidates. To do this we must know the profile of the candidate we desire and we must learn who are the players within our marketplace. Remember the section titled "competition" within the chapter on marketing tools. Recruiting represents another reason to learn about the competition.

Once you have identified potential candidates it is also important to upgrade your knowledge of them over a period of time before you start the formal recruitment process. Interviews are not the most effective means of gathering information. Start with a networking meeting. In a networking meeting you can ask questions not possible in an interview. Keeping in touch over a period of time will help you develop a relationship. Talking with people that know your prospects in a more neutral setting is also more effective than reference checking.

Integration of activities . . .

We have already identified what activities occupy the greatest portion of a manager's working day: personal production and supervision of present employees. Now we must identify actions that will help us meet recruitment objectives and increase personal and company production. We must also identify actions that will help us increase our supervisory capacity.

To illustrate this point, let us take a few examples:

1. Most sales managers hold periodic sales meetings. Far too many managers complain that these meetings degenerate into complaint sessions (*why are our prices too high?*) and far too many salespeople complain that these meetings do not help further their sales objectives. Perhaps we are spending too much time focusing on problems and products. How much time does the manager spend focusing on the company's number one objective: attracting top notch sales and operations personnel? Do you ask each salesperson to help you recruit every week and entice them with incentives? When your sales force becomes part of your recruitment plan, they are forced to start focusing on the positives within their environment. It also helps solidify their own loyalty, because they will have a vested interest in helping their recruits succeed. Why recruit alone when you could have a recruitment team of several members working in concert to meet your objectives?

2. One of the major goals of business is to learn about your competition. Your objectives for interviewing your clients and prospects should always include several questions regarding whom they are presently using, whom their peers use, what level of service they receive and more. What better way to benchmark potential recruits than by in-depth interviews with your clients. If their report is glowing, you have a recruitment target. If their report is not so glowing, you have a great opportunity to obtain more business.

These examples sufficiently illustrate how we can link the two most time consuming elements of a manager's day with the number one objective—recruitment. Of course, before we go about implementing these solutions, we must have a clear idea of our recruitment objectives. All too often we recruit anyone who is available—blindly—and wind up adding bodies instead of upgrading our staff.

When we open our eyes to take full advantage of the concept of synergy, there will be no end to the possibilities. Any action that helps us meet more than one objective will decrease our stress levels because they help us conserve our most precious resource—time. Any upgrading of our staff will also help decrease our stress levels. An excellent resource for a more comprehensive treatment of the recruitment process, especially from the viewpoint of assessing a candidate, is *Hiring The Best* by Martin Yate (Bob Adams, inc., 1994).

Reference checking—your key to making a right decision

Reference checking is as essential as the interview process in determining whether you have the right person. It may be even more important as it represents the only "independent" verification of your choice. If you do not select the right person, your management endeavors will not be successful. Here are a few guidelines:

◆ *Check at least one reference first.* Why interview someone and then find out they do not meet your requirements through their references? What a waste of time! The references you check should also give you a basis for the questions you ask during the interview.

◆ *Be polite—ask for a few minutes.* You will not get a good reference if you interrupt them at a busy time and start firing questions.

◆ *Getting a call returned.* If you reach their voice mail, indicate that you were referred by the candidate (by name) but do not give the reason for the call. If you are a potential prospect, you are more likely to get a return call. There is also the possibility that someone else will pick up the voice mail message and that person should not be privy to this confidential information.

◆ *Check independently.* Of course, they are going to list those who will give them the best reference. Check independently with your sources—vendors, competitors, etc. Ask about obvious references they have not listed (such as their supervisor at a previous company). Why did they not list them?

◆ A*sk direct, open-ended questions.* If the questions are too general or too closed, this gives the reference a chance to avoid giving out negative information. If you don't ask, they will not offer.

◆ *Don't forget synergy.* If the reference works for a competitor, ask questions that will give you information to use in your business. References represent another source of referrals. In other words, ask if they know someone else who might fill this particular position (or others).

◆ *If you get a bad reference.* Do not eliminate the candidate without getting the full story. Is it possible that the reference would also like to hire the candidate and is trying to throw you off the trail? Always give the candidate the benefit of the doubt—but the reference information must remain confidential so you will have to "probe" independently.

◆ *Make a decision promptly.* Do not give the candidate an indication that you are an indecisive leader from the beginning of the process. If you have to delay, call and tell them why.

◆ *If you decide against them.* Do not eliminate them from your life. Your best candidate later may be your second choice today. If they never hear from you, they will not respond later. We are not talking about a form letter at this juncture, but a personal phone call.

◆ *After checking, put the offer in writing.* You demonstrate your professionalism by using an offer letter that outlines all terms of the agreement. How many prospective employees change their mind after the offer is extended? You minimize this chance by having them sign the commitment.

Here are some reference questions that provoke thought and a more thorough discussion of the candidate's qualifications.

◆ Instead of, "*The candidate said they left because . . .*" try, "*The candidate indicates that they learned a lot from you during their*

173

employment. In your opinion, how did they progress in their position?" Even if the candidate thought the company or manager was terrible, you will only get them to open up to you with praise.

♦ Instead of, *"Did the candidate leave on good terms,"* try, *"Was the separation handled professionally? How could it have been handled better?"*

♦ Instead of, *"Were they a good employee,"* try, *"What were the employee's responsibilities? How well did they handle each of these?"* Be more specific, even as you are being open-ended.

♦ Instead of, *"Did they get along with other employees,"* try, *"Was the employee able to integrate as part of the team? How did they help the team?"*

♦ Instead of, *did you have any problems with ethics or fraud,* try, *if I give you a list of characteristics, please let me know how strong the candidate is from this perspective.* Do not expect them to answer tough questions directly—you must probe.

Interviewing—just part of a longer process

We have already established that the keys to management are simple.

Hire the right people;
Agree on the responsibilities;
Give them the right tools;
Get out of the way; and,
Fire your mistakes quickly.

If this is true, the interview process is crucial in getting the first step right. If you do not hire the right people, then there is no way you will be successful as a manager. Here are a few rules that will help you make the interview step "an important part" of this success.

♦ *Always require a resume ahead of time.* If you want to hire professionals, reviewing a resume can help you with the evaluation process. Do not hesitate to hire a resume verification service as it has been estimated that more than 40 percent of resumes contain falsehoods.

♦ *You still must sell—even if you are listening.* Give them a professionally prepared information package (recruitment package) on your company. Include information on the organization, products, marketing materials, benefits and more. If you want to attract professionals, your materials and presentation must be professional.

◆ *Conduct the interview in a neutral place, preferably off-site or in a conference room.* You can't listen if you are at your desk with your projects staring you in the face and your phone ringing. You also don't want your staff banging at your door with fires during this essential time.

◆ *Allow enough time—do not schedule meetings before and after.* Do not schedule interviews back-to-back on the hour. If you really want to learn about the candidate, do not rush the process.

◆ *Build your questions around your objectives.* If you place a high priority upon a particular skill, for example a team approach, then build questions to ferret out information regarding this skill.

◆ *Ask questions, do not talk.* If you really want to impress the candidate and learn something, do not sell by talking. Listen, listen, listen. Ask open-ended questions. Not *"Did you like your last job,"* but *"What did you like about your last job?"*

◆ *Use your maximum synergy rules.* Accomplish more than one objective from the interview. Other objectives may include learning more about your competition (pricing, product, marketing and compensation information) and procuring other referrals from the candidate.

◆ *Never offer the job at the interview.* No matter how impressive they are, this move reeks of unprofessionalism and will turn many candidates off.

◆ *Schedule at least one other interview before an offer is proffered.* Have another employee participate to get a second opinion (an excellent management training tool). Make sure all questions are answered from the candidate's perspective.

Here are some further pointers to turn boring, mundane closed interview questions into open-ended probes that will give you a better perspective on the individual you are considering. Note that some questions can be too broad— and we try in some cases to direct their thoughts to our objectives.

◆ *"Are you a team player?"* Instead ask, *"What have you done to contribute to team building in the past?"*

◆ *"How do you feel about being on commission?"* Instead, *"What aspects of being on commission do you like? What aspects do you not like?"*

- ◆ *"What is your education level?"* Instead, *"How has your education helped prepare you for a career in sales?"*
- ◆ *"Are you a good writer?"* Instead, *"What ways do you communicate with your prospects? How could you improve your communication skills?"*
- ◆ *"How are you at taking direction?"* Instead, *"What is the best way for a manager to get you to follow his/her lead?"*
- ◆ *"When can you start?* Instead, *Have you made a definitive decision to leave your present position and why?"*
- ◆ *"What are you looking for in a company?"* Instead, *"If you were to open a company today, what do you feel are the three most important attributes this company would have to possess to keep your employees happy?"*

Finally, do not be afraid to challenge them. We are not talking about standardized tests here—though we are also not saying that standardized tests are not advisable.

- ◆ Ask them what books they have read on a particular topic such as sales. What have they learned from these books?
- ◆ Probe statements on their resume, such as *"produced 100 percent increase in sales."* Where did they start? How does their new level rank to others within their peer group?

Ask them how they would handle a certain objection. How many times have you hired an experienced salesperson and then found they were lacking in sales skills? Do not hesitate to inject a little role playing into the interview.

Job agreements and the company mission

After hiring the right person, it is a manager's responsibility to communicate the responsibilities of the job. Most job descriptions are not very helpful in defining someone's responsibilities—especially a salesperson. They are too general and do not contain the specific information necessary to pinpoint their path to success.

As an example, most job descriptions include general statements such as "provide excellent customer service," without defining just what excellent customer service represents. We assume our employees will be able to define excellent service and then deliver the same. This statement is much too broad and leaves too much latitude in the hands of many who would define the concept in their own way. This is not to say that employees should not be involved in the definition process. They should be integral to this process. However, standards must be set for the organization.

It is at this juncture that I can give my opinion of most mission statements that are purported to be essential by so many management and business coaches. The objectives brought forward within these mission statements are even broader than most job descriptions. They remind me of statements made by politicians during a political campaign. All politicians are for a stronger defense, reduction in crime, efficiency in government, etc. No arguments here. All companies are for maximum profitability, excellent customer service, delivering value, etc. The question here is how are we going to define these concepts. Because of this broadness, most mission statements are not worth the paper upon which they are written. What is important is our actions, not our theory.

Here are a few suggestions on how best to succeed when dealing with the second most important management rule:

◆ *Responsibilities must be defined up front.* The process should start during the interview. There should be no surprises once a salesperson or other employee starts on the job.

◆ *Start with a two-way agreement.* This agreement should cover their goals for the first 30 days and once they will achieve "full production" levels. It should include what support will be needed from the company to accomplish the job. Most importantly, the individual goals must be related to the company's goals. For example, if the type of business brought in by the salesperson cannot be supported by the inside staff, the new production might actually slow the company's progress.

◆ *Get specific in many areas.* The agreement must include a statement on what administrative responsibilities are required— including attendance at sales meetings, required reports, level of customer service follow-up, and overall product mix. General statements such as "follow directions" will not help guide anyone later in the process. If they are to deliver excellent service what does that mean?

- How quickly are they to respond to phone calls?
- How many times will they follow-up after the sale?
- What progress reports are they required to give?
- What additional value must they deliver?
- What steps are to be taken in response to complaints?

♦ *Make sure the agreement is in writing.* Putting the responsibilities in writing avoids problems later on. How many times have you sat down with an underachiever and they did not admit their production was not adequate? The agreement might include the following facets:

- production levels;
- individual marketing efforts;
- quality of production;
- profitability of production;
- customer service delivery;
- teamwork; and,
- communication.

If you are truly interested in more productivity with less stress, then you will take the time necessary to avoid supervisory nightmares. Managers cannot be effective if the salespeople they are supervising do not know in which direction to move in order to achieve the long-term goals of the organization. The long-term goals must be specific and clear—and not communicated in the form of a general mission statement.

Coaching for success

When a salesperson is not producing it sometimes can be very difficult to discover the reasons for the lack of production. The possible explanations for lack of success can be as varied as the sales situations that sales personnel face each and every day. Here are just a few:

♦ Perhaps they are not confident in their knowledge level;
♦ Perhaps they are not making enough calls;
♦ Perhaps they are not calling on the right targets;
♦ Perhaps they are not saying the right things to the right targets;
♦ Perhaps they are not asking for the business;
♦ Perhaps they are not making adjustments when one approach does not work; or,
♦ Perhaps their approach is not professional.

Assuming that the salesperson has a high level of desire for success and is acting on that desire, the salesperson may be as confused about their lack of success as their manager. How do they know what they are doing wrong? One fact that we do know—if they are not making adjustments every day, success will not follow.

One approach would be to attempt field-coaching calls—i.e., accompany the salesperson out in the field (for telemarketers this is easier, because we can monitor phone calls). The manager might attempt any combination of three types of coaching calls:

◆ *A training call.* In this call, the manager performs a sales call and the salesperson simply observes. This might be accomplished before the salesperson's client or the manager's client—if the manager is a producing manager.

◆ *A laboratory or coaching call.* In this call, the manager simply observes the salesperson in action, trying to interject nothing—or as little as possible.

◆ *A joint call.* In this call, the manager calls on a target with the salesperson. This might typically take place when the target is a previous customer of the manager or the manager is going to do a presentation at the client's sales meeting.

The only type of call that is designed to tell us what the salesperson is doing wrong is a coaching call. Unfortunately, we are not in a laboratory situation. As soon as a manager is on the street with or listening to a salesperson, the salesperson will tend to modify his or her behavior to match what he/she thinks the manager wants.

Finding the time for effective coaching is difficult, especially with producing sales managers. Maximum synergy rules dictate that our actions will need to achieve more than one objective. Therefore, producing managers should integrate their coaching into their own production process. An excellent example would be to take a rookie out on sales calls. Why leave them at the office observing when they could be out in the field?

It is important to note that all salespeople need some type of coaching—even those who are successful. Those who are very successful may need help in achieving another goal such as becoming managers themselves. Your top producers can help you coach, saving you precious time and becoming part of the management training process. Maximum synergy rules require that you use all of your present resources to achieve your objectives.

Coaching must be consistent. It should not only occur when the salesperson is underachieving. In some situations, monthly or even weekly coaching may be required. At a minimum it should be accomplished quarterly. An annual review is not the same as coaching. We will address reviews in a later section. Do not assume that all sales personnel must have coaching sessions at the same frequency. Also, the type of coaching should vary. Field calls should be interspersed with inside one-on-one meetings. No matter what the frequency, you must give your undivided attention. If you must leave the office to accomplish individual meetings—do so. At the least, utilize the conference room. Schedule the next session as soon as this one ends—do not wait until you have free time (schedule section).

Sales meetings—a true opportunity for synergy applications

Does this scene look familiar to you?

It is Thursday morning. A sales meeting is scheduled for 9:00 am. A few salespeople are present early, but a few more wander in at 9:15 am. The manager gets a last minute phone call regarding a crisis. Too bad, as the manager was going to work up the agenda just before the meeting. At 9:20 am the meeting finally starts. Three pagers go off in the first ten minutes. Another gets up to get more coffee. The manager starts talking about why we haven't produced enough in the past week. The sales force responds: our prices are too high. Besides, you can't process the business we have. Within 15 minutes, the meeting digresses into a complaint session with a capital "B." No one looks forward to the next meeting—least of all the manager.

Sales meetings should be the ultimate tool for sales managers, yet many times we underutilize this tool or worse turn it into a tool of destruction. We get so busy fighting fires and the competition that we do not spend enough time preventing the same. The absolute best way to prevent fires is to provide the training necessary to adequately prepare our employees. In today's business world we usually cannot find the time to train on a continual basis. Yet t is not unusual to dedicate time weekly to sales meetings that turn out to be not as productive as they should be. So why not use these meetings as a training vehicle? Training is a significant tool managers should provide to help their employees do their job.

The very name—*sales meeting*—implies that we are holding a meeting to help improve the sales of our team. There is no way that we are going to improve our sales techniques by concentrating on what is not working, which tends to be the focus of many weekly meetings. For example, *what is the company not providing us or what are the salespeople not doing right*? For sales meetings to be successful, we need to concentrate on what is working and how we can instill this success within all of our producers. Here are a few examples of what skills could be imparted within a sales meeting and what delivery vehicles might be utilized.

◆ *Product knowledge.* The most common training component of sales meetings regards the introduction of products. In some respects, this focus makes sense because we all know that salespeople must have excellent product knowledge in order to become more proficient. Our concentration and delivery methods sometimes leads much to be desired. Does your coverage of a new product entail reading the pertinent specifications in the meeting? Boring! Focus of the features and benefits that will help your staff increase their sales. Then deliver it in a way that will benefit each and every one of them. Perhaps you could ask a salesperson to deliver a sales presentation based upon the new product. Now you are training on a new product and combining this with presentation training. Another method would be to hold a role-playing exercise. This will make the meeting much more interactive!

◆ *Public presentation skills.* Public speaking skills may be the most important of presentation skills. There is nothing more effective than being able to deliver a dynamite presentation in front of ten or more potential targets. How many cold calls or lunches would it take to achieve the same level of impact? Of course, we do know that public speaking skills do not happen overnight. They happen with many weeks, months and even years of practice. What better practice vehicle then the weekly sales meeting? Too busy to come up with an agenda each week? Have one of your originators hold the meeting! As an alternative, schedule a practice presentation each week during the meeting. In other words, get everyone involved.

◆ *Individual presentation skills.* Managing salespeople is especially difficult because so much of their success is due to what they say and to whom they say it *out on the street or on the phone.* The best manager cannot be out on coaching calls every minute of the day. In many industries, managers are producing sales managers and spend precious little time out on the street with their staff. Sales meetings make an excellent opportunity to set up role-playing exercises. If you want the meeting to be fun and interactive there is no better way to achieve it than setting up real life situations. There is also no harder audience than your peers. In other words, if your sales force can cut the mustard in front of their peers, they will be much more confident out on the street—or on the phones.

◆ *Benchmarking*. The key to any successful sales event is concentrating upon what is right. We do that through the process of benchmarking. This key concept involves discovering the practices of successful entities and sharing it with others. There is no reason to completely reinvent the wheel to increase our level of production. There are examples of success within your own office, other branches within your company and other companies. Try bringing in a guest from another branch (or another company— either a "friendly" competitor, vendor or target) to share what they know. The last thing your staff wants to hear is their manager telling them what is right again and again.

◆ *Articles*. Include sales related articles each week. Have one of the participants comment upon and/or present the article. How does this article relate to your current sales situations and challenges? How might we deliver these articles to our targets so that we might become more value-added? Might the article be a basis for a sales presentation we can deliver? Subscribe to industry specific publications and general sales periodicals so that you constantly have a stream of fresh material and ideas.

The ideas we could bring forth regarding using the sales meeting as a sales training vehicle are endless. How many times has your sales meeting become bogged down in the details of problems indicative to your industry as a whole as opposed to a breeding ground for ideas designed to scale the challenges brought forth by your industry? The first step moving in the direction of the latter is to make a decision regarding the objectives of your sales meeting. Your commitment to the objective of training is the first step of what could be a long and rewarding process. And don't forget maximum synergy rule number one— accomplishing more objectives with one activity. If recruiting is a major goal, how can the sales meetings be structured to help with your recruiting process?

Training—essential, but can we deliver?

The third rule of management is to give your employees the tools they need to produce. After you hire the right people and let them know their job, they must have the tools necessary to accomplish their responsibilities. There is no more important tool than training. It is not unusual for salespeople not to be trained regularly or effectively—even if the company has the best of intentions.

◆ *The two faces training*. It is important to recognize that there are two types of training. Field training is discussed within the coaching section. Since many managers are producers and do not have the time to train, it makes sense to have trainees accompany them in the field (or onto phone calls) so that the manager can accomplish two goals at once. The second type of training occurs in the "class room." An example of classroom training is discussed within the sales meeting section. Sales meetings are an excellent way of promoting regular training. Good training systems employ both methods of instruction.

◆ *Learning on the job*. This is the way the need to focus upon "learn while you earn" is usually communicated—*the only way you can learn this job is by doing it*. It is true that field training is very important and provides specific advantages over classroom settings. For example, the one-on-one time out in the field may enable a manager to create a closer bond with a new salesperson. However, administered as the entire training program, *learning on the job* is not effective and one should not be in a position of being dependent upon this one-dimensional tool. We can always supplement *on the job training* with courses, books and other available resources.

◆ *Determine the need*. It is not solely up to the manager or the company to make a determination as to what training is necessary at a particular point in time. You must probe your sales staff and even your targets to make a full determination of needs. It is not unusual for sales training to be focused substantially or even entirely on product knowledge. It is true that specific product knowledge is important. It is just as true that sales skills such as presentations skills, listening skills and more are just as important with regard to the fulfillment of training needs to the responsibilities of the position.

◆ *Resources*. Because resources such as time are limited, synergy rules dictate that we utilize all effective tools available when developing our training programs. This includes all resources within the organization. For example, senior sales personnel can share their "on the job" expertise and this participation imparts skills to help facilitate senior personnel development. Quite often vendors of companies will provide training resources, either through the vendors delivering their own programs or the hiring of outside trainers. Local colleges and other commercial schools offer classes on-line or within classrooms that can be worked into the overall training curriculum for the company. Each industry will also have an association or associations that will provide a training resource

◆ *Orientation*. Training should start with a full orientation as to the organization of the company, functions of different divisions of the company, specific responsibilities of the position, marketing and operational support available, etc. Orientation should not consist of a couple of days "wandering" around the office.

◆ *Consistency.* Training must be delivered consistently. It should not be delivered only when a major need is discovered (profits or sales are falling) or when it is mandated by human resources personnel (time for the annual sexual harassment training). This is why we must integrate training into our everyday routine such as weekly sales meetings and field visits—using maximum synergy. To help you achieve this consistency without sacrificing your own efficiency you will have to have the help of veterans within your organization. This assistance will become part of their management training curriculum, again making maximum use of synergy opportunities.

◆ *Create Buddies.* Especially with sales personnel reporting to producing managers, we do not have the time to keep everyone as focused as we would like. Pairing up salespeople according to experience, geography and product lines can produce some interesting synergies. Buddy systems can be informal or formalized within compensation structures. They can be structured to help achieve several goals including management training and cross selling.

◆ *Cross Training.* Every organization becomes more effective if their employees are integrated into the overall goals of the company. Cross training may include training salespeople to sell different products within the company (cross-selling), training salespeople to help within operations or training operations personnel to help recognize sales opportunities. There is no better synergy than having all aspects of your organization working together so that they can achieve more than one objective with their present activities. Especially as companies become larger, the cross-selling opportunities become larger and more crucial. My experience as a member of the board of directors of a bank selling mortgages, insurance, brokerage services and more has made me keenly aware of how difficult it can be to make personnel aware of all synergies between different divisions of the organization.

Cross training also gives each employee skills that will make them more valuable to the company and to future employers at various stages of their career. If we deliver extra value to our employees, they become more loyal and more productive members of the organization. True synergy represents the delivery of value and nothing can be more significant than the value we deliver to our most important assets.

Delegation

If ever there was a management skill that was essential for the effective implementation of synergy for management, sales, marketing or customer service, it is the *art of delegation*. We call it an art because delegation is a tough skill to master. Some do not have the constitution to give up a delegable task and others delegate and do so in such a clumsy manner that they would have been better not delegating at all.

First, let us deal with the psychological issue. Delegating will not make a manager seem lazy to their subordinates. Delegating well is a leadership quality that evokes admiration. Don't think that Donald Trump was ever berated for not typing his merger agreements. Your subordinates must realize that you delegate for the following reasons:

- You delegate tasks that fit the skill sets of others better than yourself. Not being able to program a computer does not make you a poor manager.
- You delegate tasks that free you up for other priorities. If you are delegating so that you can play golf every day, this is a problem.
- You delegate tasks because in the long run the project may be handled by another arm of the organization. An earlier handoff may expedite the process for a prospect or customer.
- You delegate tasks because it helps your subordinates gain the skills necessary for growth.

Second, let us deal with the method of delegation. Effective delegation does not involve throwing a project on someone's desk and saying *handle it*. Often it is not the act of delegation that causes resentment, it is how we go about communicating delegated tasks. Effective delegation involves transferring the information necessary to effect the task—including the steps that must be taken and the expected results and timeframe.

Effective delegation also involves:

- The explanation of the reason for delegation, the priority of the project and where it might lead in the long run;
- Making sure the person receiving the delegation has the right skill set to complete the task;
- Delegating the authority to make decisions to complete the project; and,

◆ Letting go completely when it is appropriate—do not look over someone's shoulder.

Why is delegation so important with regard to the implementation of synergy?

◆ Delegation helps you impart skills to your employees. Delegating management responsibilities such as orientation, coaching and training helps others achieve management skills. All too often we promote employees to management positions and then wonder why they do not have supervisory skills. Effective delegation can also help us with our cross-training goals. One action, more than one result . . .

◆ Delegation helps you select priorities rather than react to priorities. Synergy requires that we chose the most effective targets and tools. We cannot do this if we cannot chose our path from minute to minute because we are fighting fires. Want to call the present customers and ask for referrals? Can't do such because your office is changing computer systems or moving? What can be delegated so that you can achieve both goals?

Sales incentives/contests

The use of sales contests or other incentive programs in order to promote the achievement of individual and team goals is as *old as the hills* in the world of business. Most individual sales compensation plans are incentive laden and a whole industry exists that caters to the fulfillment of incentives such as trips or other premiums. There is no doubt about the fact that these sales incentives are meant to help us achieve our goals. Yet, when they become commonplace, there can be substantial doubt as to the efficacy of the method versus the results. If a salesperson wins an all-expenses paid trip they are going to laud the practice. Yet, would they have reached the same level with or without the trip as an incentive? Could they have achieved additional goals with a different set of criteria? Would it have achieved more sales if the company incited the salesperson with a cash bonus?

Synergy must be an integral part of incentive planning. Incentive planning is really about the achievement of more results with limited resources and the selection of the most effective tool within a varied arsenal. Here are a few considerations to help us integrate synergy throughout this process.

Goal planning. We must have a clear idea of our goals in order to make incentive planning successful. If we set standards year-after-year based upon last year's achievement levels plus ten percent, pretty soon we have a nice incentive program that is not linked to company goals. Synergy rule number one dictates that we try to achieve more than one goal from the same action. If we clearly link our goals to the incentive we may very well achieve more from our incentive program. For example:

◆ If our goal is to increase the quality of sales, does our incentive have a quality component as well as a volume target?

◆ If our goal is to incite the sale of a particular product or level of sales, how can these products or services be highlighted within the program?

◆ If our goal is to increase our recruitment efforts, how can we incite our sales and/or operations team to become part of the process? Perhaps if an operations team member successfully recruits a salesperson, they will be the "guest" of that salesperson the first year they win a trip.

◆ If our goal is to increase sales through higher levels of customer service or through cross-selling, how can we incite our inside staff accordingly?

Use more than one tool. Having a President's *Club Gala* at the end of the year does not preclude using other incentive tools. Too often we utilize our entire incentive budget through these trips and as a result we lose the ability to achieve additional goals throughout the year. This is not intended to be an argument against large, expensive trips. It is intended to make us aware of the fact that incentives should be continuous and not a *one-shot make-it-or-stay-home alternative.*

Many incentives such as recognition need not be expensive. For example, the top salesperson or top customer service representative might:

◆ have lunch with the CEO;

◆ be given an employee of the month plaque or parking space;

◆ be written-up in the company newsletter;

◆ be given an additional marketing allowance for the month; or,

◆ be approved to take a course.

Note the last two examples are of incentives that enable the winner to increase their business levels even further. This is what synergy is all about. Cash prizes may spur action, but they cannot leverage that action. The question is—how does the achievement of your company's incentive award help the winner increase their business even more?

The existence of smaller, more focused incentives not only enables a more immediate focus (program of the month) but also allows you to have categories or tiers to include more participation. Contests may be set for operations personnel, new sales personnel or those selling a certain product line.

Use synergy partnerships. Many companies are not able to budget for the type of incentives they would like because of expense considerations. Yet, there are vendors who consistently strive for more intimate access to members of the company's sales force and cannot achieve such because there is not enough time.

Perhaps you are a large insurance brokerage and the vendor represents one of the insurance companies delivering a product your company sells. You would like for your agents to sell more of their policies but you don't have the time to provide intimate product training. That insurance company might actually pay to be a part of your large incentive trip. This achieves the dual goal of off-setting part of the cost of the trip and providing necessary product training. Many vendors will also provide sales trainers or other speakers on a regular basis for such events.

Be flexible. While there is much to be said regarding a consistent incentive program from year-to-year, unless we evaluate and adjust in accordance with changing market conditions, products, targets and goals, it is unlikely we will have the most effective incentive program possible. For some situations individual incentives are important. At other times team goals can be more effective. What works today may not work tomorrow. This is why the evaluation is so important when implementing any synergistic activity. We cannot add additional doses of synergy unless we are constantly striving for the achievement of additional objectives.

The review

If we follow our rules of management religiously by hiring the right people, giving them the tools to do their job and getting out of their way, our perspective regarding reviews will change significantly. Whether we decide to accomplish reviews weekly, monthly, quarterly or annually, in the real world reviews typically become the vehicles in which we deliver negative feedback we did not deliver day-to-day. In other words, reviews are likely to become negative experiences rather than part of the process in which we deliver valuable tools to our employees.

In many cases reviews are done sporadically when a need arises instead of with a clear plan of progressive value for the employee. I have consistently counseled managers who have indicated that they *need to have a review with this employee to set them straight* (or as a precursor to dismissal). Employees then react negatively to reviews because it is demonstrated that reviews have a negative connotation. We have already established that coaching must be accomplished with regularity and in connection with the achievement of everyday tasks. Synergy rules dictate that we integrate our coaching activities into our everyday routine so that we can consistently accomplish more than one task at once.

Therefore, reviews must be carried out regularly and with a goal of delivering value to our employees. They do not have to be separate and distinct from the process of everyday coaching but the goals of each must be met. How do we deliver value to our employees? We can do this by learning their goals and setting out plans to achieve these goals. This means that reviews must be utilized for garnering feedback from the employee. Like any other facet of successful communication we accomplish this task by asking questions and listening. Ultimate synergy is represented by the delivery of value and we cannot determine how to deliver value without a needs assessment.

What type of questions might you ask? Here are a few examples:

◆ Have you determined what is the best way for you to help achieve the company's goals?

◆ Where would you like to be in the organization in the next few years?

◆ What skills do you feel you need to improve and how can we help you improve these skills?

◆ What opportunities do you see to improve the organization?

◆ Are you satisfied as to what you have accomplished?

◆ How could you serve your customers better? How could the company better help you accomplish this?

◆ How could we work together better as a team?

Of course, the evolution of the review process from sporadic negative coaching sessions to positive value delivery segments requires strict adherence to the first and most important rule of management. If you do not hire the right people, your management world will be filled with fighting fires and you will never be in a position to deliver value. This means that you must make the appropriate use of the synergy tools previously introduced—including recruiting, interviewing and reference checking.

There are opportunities to integrate synergy into our review process in other ways. Synergy rules dictate that there are always ways to add additional synergy from our present tasks. For example, many organizations take great care to garner feedback from their customers regarding their present and future needs and present levels of satisfaction regarding service delivery from the company. This may be accomplished through written surveys, face-to-face via the telephone. Why not have the customer give a review of a sales or customer service person's performance? Perhaps we can ask how well the salesperson understands the needs of the customer. What opinion would be more important than that of our customer? Wouldn't this put us in better position to deliver more value to our customers? Vendors can also give us another perspective on our employees.

Once again, this feedback should not be used in a way that would build up negative data in order for it to be unleashed as part of an annual review. The feedback should be part of the regular coaching process. As in any coaching process, the negative feedback must be accompanied with positive statements. Within the feedback process, you will find that employees will magnify negative feedback at least three times. In other words, to give an equal review you must make three positive comments for every negative comment. Blanchard and Johnson in *The One Minute Manager* (Berkley Publishing Group, 1983) indicates that appreciation is the number one tool any manager can use for effectiveness. Becoming a great coach helping people achieve their goals rather than a manager who manages tasks and the people accomplishing these tasks is a worthy goal of leaders. An excellent treatment of this concept can be found in *Stop Managing, Start Coaching*, by Gilley and Boughton, Irwin Professional Publishing, 1996.

Conflict management—opportunity for leadership

Conflict is never something we look forward to as a salesperson, manager or customer service employee. In today's fast paced world it is always inevitable. Unfortunately, in today's fast paced world it is sometimes the most time consuming and stress related activity in our lives. We spend entirely too much time fighting fires and dealing with situations that need to be fixed. These activities prevent us from effectively using our resources and creating synergy.

Conflicts typically occur because of a lack of clear communication up-front. As a manager we might not fully understand the skills of an employee or clearly communicate the responsibilities of the job. We may not learn the needs of a customer or we may promise something we cannot deliver. As a rule, the management of conflict should start before conflict occurs—when it can be prevented.

Leaders as opposed to managers use advanced communication skills to bring a conflict to resolution. Whether clearly enunciating a policy or meeting with two disgruntled employees (or a customer), the leader can guide us to a situation in which all parties feel they have been heard and something will be done to resolve the conflict.

Follow-up is very important in resolving conflicts. Too many times we promise to change something and then do not make sure the action we promised is accomplished. A conflict will not go away—it will only grow larger and more contentious especially after we have fueled the fire with more promises. If we do follow-up we have the chance to make an aggrieved customer or employee our advocate.

The real leader recognizes when we have violated rule number one of management—hire the right person. If the person we have hired (or the customer we have taken on) cannot help us meet our goals, we must sever the ties quickly. This is against our human nature because we feel as managers we can just fix things or the person will improve. This is why we are stressed much of the time. Conflict management takes too much of our most precious resource—time. It also adds too much stress to our lives. Getting rid of the root of the problem quickly is our most beneficial synergy action. The ability to reverse our poor decisions quickly and decisively represents the ultimate synergy tool.

CHAPTER SEVEN
Leveraging Customer Service For
More Productivity With Less Stress

"If you would like to predict the future, change it."
Peter Drucker

Time and time again we have made the point that true synergy begins with the leverage of one's existing relationships. The most stressful thing we can ever do is to start the sales process over and over again without leveraging the precious resources we have expended yesterday, last week and every year we have been in business.

Of course, this leverage can only take place with the delivery of great customer service. Ten years of a great economy and the massive application of technology have put a great strain on the labor markets within America and in many areas the levels of customer service we have experienced have gotten worse. This is the same technology that keeps producing more economic productivity and fueling our growth without inflation. In essence, we are producing more goods with less people and these same reduced work forces have to handle more and more customers. What has been great for the economy in not necessarily good for individuals as we strain their limits. More productivity for the economy, but more stress for individuals. This is why synergy is so important.

It was less than a decade ago that we were hailing the progress brought to us by premium customer service organizations such as Nordstroms and Ritz-Carlton. As a matter of fact, *The Nordstrom Way* (Spector & McCarthy, Wiley 1995) became a best seller and many thought we were moving as a country in the direction of elevating the importance of service within our economy. "Shoppers," were hired to come in (or call) and assess the customer service skills of retail and service organizations. Then came the age of the Internet and the ability of skeleton staffs to reach millions of people with one concept—lower prices and speed. Profit margins per transaction are down in every industry and each person must handle more and more transactions in order to survive. This applies whether you are a lawyer or an airline.

What we have accomplished is a lowered expectation of customers in America. While this can be seen as a negative, it is really an opportunity for the average business person. Those who deliver great customer service and easily exceed the expectations of their clients will prosper. As companies become larger and larger through mergers and the application of technology and cut staff, there is an opportunity for individual business people to step-up and differentiate themselves. The banking industry is an excellent example. Larger banks are merging and merging and providing an opportunity for smaller banks with personal customer service to prosper. And the cycle continues.

There is no way you can deliver this service without finding the time necessary within this demanding economic environment. The application of our maximum synergy rules are essential in order to survive in a world that expects more productivity. We can advance all the technology in the word, but our time constraints will remain the same as the demands of our targets continue to grow.

Customer service—start the leverage now

Most people in business wonder why they don't get more referrals. Their managers wonder why they don't ask more often. Are they afraid of failure? Not really. If they don't ask, they are sure to fail! One reason they don't ask is that they do not feel worthy. One reason they may not feel worthy is because they have not delivered *golden customer service*. Anytime we do a great job, referrals just begin to flow naturally.

Following is a summary of five ideas that will just about help everyone deliver better customer service and garner more referrals:

Deliver more than is expected. Great customer service does not result from a customer who receives the service they expected to receive. It results from a customer who expected great service but received more than he/she expected. This means that we delivered great value. Great value does not emanate from lowering your prices. It comes from adding benefits. This value may be derived from an effort to educate your customer through seminars, articles or newsletters or it may be derived from making their lives more comfortable or more productive.

In this day and age, your customers' expectations may have been lowered just enough to surprise them with an "extra" dose of service. How can this be effected? On the follow page are a few additional ways to set up your organization to deliver more than is expected.

♦ Eliminate what the customer doesn't want to hear—such as *"it is not my job"* or *"you need to speak to another department."*

♦ Replace the same with statements such as *"perhaps I can get someone on the line who can do even a better job of resolving your situation than myself."*

♦ Communicate to the whole organization what customers are saying—both good and bad. Feedback, whether formalized within surveys or ad hoc, is worthless unless the communication is effected in such a way that reinforcement and adjustments can be made.

♦ If you believe in the *"Nordstrom"* or *"Ritz-Carlton"* ways, we will delegate to our employees the authority *and* knowledge necessary to resolve customer situations. Delegation should be designed to deal with more than specific customer "situations." The more we delegate, the more employees are empowered. The more our employees are empowered, the more satisfied they are likely to be. Satisfied employees are more likely to deliver top-notch customer service.

♦ Focus less on being right and more on meeting our customers' needs. This means listening carefully to their statements and body language. This process may be formalized through such vehicles such as customer focus groups and advisory boards—or one-on-one. In this way you are actually empowering your customers as well as your employees. You can find excellent examples of this technique demonstrated by several major corporations in *Keeping the Edge* by Dick Schaaf (1995, Penguin Books).

Don't promise more than you can deliver. If you promise more than you can deliver you will never—we repeat never—exceed your customers' expectations. We are constantly pressured to make promises we can't keep:

"I can deliver that car saturday."
"I can sell the property at that price."

Those who overpromise are basically being dishonest to get the business in the door. Their sales skills are no sharper than those who rely upon cut-rates to bring in business. Cut-rate or cut-throat? The result will be the same.

Don't set your service up for failure. How might one set their service up for failure? For one thing, try settling all your business (such as delivering cars) on the last day of the month. Be assured that a last day of the month settlement for everyone will carry the memory of an insane experience. Your customer wants to spend an extra hour trying to learn the satellite system? Try getting an extra hour from any personnel at the dealership!

If you know you are going to have a problem within the process, set up systems that may help ease the pain of your customers. For example, if a retail establishment is going to have a long wait during the holiday season (in person or over the phone), here are a few pointers:

- *Organize the wait.* The worst feeling for a customer is to wait in line for 15 minutes and then find out they were in the wrong line the whole time (or missing information necessary to consummate the transaction). This may be even more frustrating over the phone when there is no way to speak up and ask. Make sure the "lines" are clearly labeled and organized.

- *Let them know how long.* If the wait is going to be long, make this information clearly available so that the customer has the option of coming back at a later time. In addition, let them know at what times the lines are not as long to help them make that determination.

- *Give incentives to those who help.* Customers can take many actions to help the establishment with their time crunches. These can range from paying with cash to shopping during off-hours. Express lines and other incentives reward those who help the organization deliver top-notch customer service.

- *Reinforce benefits while they wait.* If you have a guarantee or other compelling offer, make sure these are reinforced while they wait to enact business. Perhaps this will not completely counteract the ill feelings they garner from the wait, but every little bit of good will helps.

- *Thank them for being patient.* Thank them in every way for being patient. If in person, display free coffee and candy. If waiting on the phone, thank them verbally and follow with a written communication.

Another way a firm might set themselves up for failure is when the customers do not understand what you mean when you make a promise. This may happen because we are not clear or we communicated at the wrong time. We must make sure we have our customer's undivided attention when we deliver our promise. Repeat your key information and ask questions to ensure they understand all aspects of the offer. Clear communication can prevent many conflicts.

When you do promise—deliver! If you said you are going to get something done, don't let it slide. Return your calls and guide people through the process. Don't refer them to operations or other personnel with whom they are not familiar. Every time you pass the baton there is the potential to lose the customer in a black hole. If you must pass the baton, pass it with personal attention and care.

When you don't deliver—don't hide! Making a mistake is never a pleasant experience. Running and hiding afterwards can make the experience a nightmare. Ninety percent of customer complaints can be turned around through apologizing afterwards and listening empathetically. Stand tall and take whatever you have coming. Offer anything you can to help make the situation right. It is said that good relationships can never become great until something goes wrong.

Are you really committed to great customer service? If you are not, then you will have to survive by starting over and over again with cold calls instead of building upon relationships. Why would anyone want the stress of customer service nightmares and drumming up new business again and again? Losing your most effective target leaves you the furthest from implementing our synergy rules.

Complaints are an opportunity to solidify your most effective target

Think back to the situations that have hurt your business in the last few years. Anyone who is in sales and delivers service has had experiences that have caused their customers to be unhappy.

Nothing is more unsettling than an unhappy customer. Well, this statement is not entirely true. Nothing is more unsettling than an unhappy customer on behalf of whom we have expended major resources and now expect to get no additional business from in return. Wasting resources is the opposite of synergy.

Nothing is more unsettling and nothing is more likely—if you don't take specific actions to rectify this situation. It is the unhappy customer who provides the perfect opportunity for more business. And in this day and age, there is no way we want to miss any opportunities.

How in the world can an unhappy customer be a source for new business? It is the customer who makes the most noise that cares the most about their relationship with you. In other words, the customers who walk away from the table unhappy but stay silent about their feelings are not likely to care about their long-term relationship with you as their service provider.

Can it be that you have missed a sales opportunity every time a customer was very unhappy with your service? When things get rough, our initial reaction is to run and hide. Instead we need to meet the customer with a heightened sense of responsibility. Here are a few pointers:

- *Listen, listen and listen.* A customer who is unhappy does not want to hear your opinion about why certain things turned out the way they did. They just want to be heard. Stop, take a deep breath and listen.

- *React calmly.* If you get excited and shoot back with accusations as to how the customer contributed to the situation (you didn't get me . . .) or how someone else in the company let you down, you will make the customer even more excited and unhappy.

- *Show empathy.* Tell the customer you understand their feelings and that you are just as disappointed as them. You must give them the distinct feeling that you feel their pain. Do not forget to tell them how important they are to you and your company. Appeal to their ego as much as possible.

- *Take action.* The customer wants more than a sympathetic ear. They would like you to make things better. Take any action possible to rectify the situation. They need to see you taking control and producing a better result—even if it is not the original result they wanted. As most customers will not be insulted by the process of compromise, this action may result in a negotiating phase.

- *Apologize.* Say you are sorry. Especially if you can't undo what has already taken place, they want to know how important it is to you that they are unhappy. A letter with a gift certificate can always underscore this fact. Or, say it with flowers!

- *Learn from lost customers.* The lessons we learn from lost customers are buried treasures says Wayne Burkan in *Wide Angle Vision* (1996, John Wyley and Sons). We cannot expect to retain all disgruntled customers (though we can try), but we can learn from all we disenfranchise.

- *Talk to those who are silent.* Do not assume silent customers are happy. Many will not care enough to speak up when they are estranged. Reach out through surveys and/or phone calls. Use probing questions such as *"is there something we could have improved within the process."*

If you follow these simple steps, you are more than likely to end up with a customer who has even greater respect for you and your company. It is often said that relationships are not solidified until there is a problem. Anyone can sell if there are no obstacles to overcome.

Before you implement new marketing plans designed to conquer new markets, let's take a step back and review the one customer base with which you are the least likely to be thinking about getting in touch. Yes, we are not only suggesting that you implement these plans for future customer mishaps—but go back in time as well.

Go back and contact those you did not face in the heat of the battle. Let them know how much their unhappiness has been on your mind and how much you have wanted to tell them how disappointed you are. Let them vent one more time and offer a token of your appreciation.

Then sit back and see if the process leads somewhere else. Don't ask for additional business or another referral. But do make clear that you know your performance in delivering top notch customer service is important to you because your business is built on referrals. Let them make the first step in this regard. You may merely feel better for making this move and make them feel better because you care. Or, you just might set yourself up for more business in the long run. In other words, source all of your previous customers, not just those who walked away happy. This might result in the delivery of true synergy.

Customer service surveys and maximum synergy marketing—the ultimate link

Maximum synergy marketing rules dictate that every marketing action can be made more effective through the use of synergy. No individual action illustrates this rule more effectively than the use of customer service surveys. Several industries utilize surveys in order to gauge their service delivery systems.

The general purpose of these surveys is to improve customer service by identifying problem incidents and areas. Ninety percent of customer service problems can be resolved by a sympathetic ear. If we don't identify those who are disgruntled we will never have the opportunity to turn these customers in our favor. Most of the time we spend following up on customer service surveys is spent correcting problems identified—and it is time well spent.

But what about the 98 percent of customer service surveys that are returned positively? Do we spend enough time focusing upon the potential benefits of utilizing these? There are opportunities that await our use of these tools when we apply synergy marketing rules.

For one, a company or individual should never advertise again without using the third party endorsements contained in these surveys. It is one thing for a salesperson to state to a prospect that they give good service. Do you think that anyone has ever approached a prospect and said: *Use me, I am mediocre!* It is quite another thing for another customer to make the same statement for you. Make sure your surveys are not all multiple choice, and give the respondent room to elaborate. A simple, *may we quote you*, box can be provided to check and this will give you permission to use these quotes. Quotes from surveys can be used in many ways:

- Put together a flyer that contains a multitude of quotes. Headline the flyer with *What The Public Is Saying . . .* or *Great Customer Service Is A Way Of Life At . . .*
- Place many of these flyers in a notebook. When a prospect asks: *"Why should I use you?"* show them concrete proof.
- Make a collage of letters, frame them and place them in the reception area of your office. If you have a storefront, enlarge the quotes and place them in your window.
- Place the quotes on your fax cover sheets.

Another use of surveys entails the garnering of referrals from our clients. Everyone agrees that we should get more referrals from previous clients. Few of us have made obtaining referrals the object of our everyday actions. To be effective in garnering more referrals we have to follow three important steps:

- We must ask for specific referrals;
- We must make it easy for the customer to give us referrals; and,
- We should offer an incentive for the customer to give us referrals.

Many teach that we should ask by stating: *I make my living off of referrals. I would appreciate if you would give me . . .* This will never be effective because of the number of "me" statements. Customer service surveys often broach the subject of referrals by stating: *Would you refer someone else to us?* This does not satisfy the first referral step: asking specifically.

To truly ask, the survey must give room for a specific response that includes a name and phone number. To make it easier, we must prompt their memory by giving examples of whom they might refer (neighbors, those they work with, etc.).

Finally we must offer an incentive for maximum effectiveness. Offer an incentive to return the survey and if it contains a referral double the prize!

What might constitute such an incentive? It does not have to be expensive. Perhaps the value can be delivered by a synergy partner. Involving your synergy marketing partner makes the action even more effective. A specific referral strategy is much more effective than giving out three business cards.

A customer service survey to increase customer service levels? A great idea. Why not a survey to increase your business as well? It is important that we end our trip through the business process—from marketing to sales to management to customer service—with a linkage back to marketing. This is what synergy is all about. If you do not link one part of the process with the other we will no way be able to produce more with less resources. Why start over when we can take our last action and build upon that action to deliver an even more effective result? Synergy lives everywhere in the process!

CONCLUSION

*"Look for your choices, pick the best one,
then go with it."*
Pat Riley

We have introduced many, many concepts during our discussion of maximum synergy. First the seven maximum synergy rules:

1. Every activity you undertake must achieve two results;
2. If you are marketing by yourself, you are wasting synergy;
3. Certain targets are more effective than others
4. Certain tools are more effective than others
5. Every action can be made more effective through additional doses of synergy
6. If there is no response mechanism, do not waste your resources
7. If you are not offering something of value to your targets, why bother?

As we have discussed the relevance of these rules we have brought forth several other concepts that will help in realizing the benefits of implementing these rules.

1. Without the attitude, don't even try implementing any part of your marketing plan.
2. Improvement comes one step at a time.
3. Improvement starts after you admit you need improvement.
4. If you don't know where you are going, how do you know you are heading in the right direction every day?
5. You will do everything else before marketing.
6. You won't be in a position to sell if you don't call.

7. You won't win if you don't play—you won't sell if you don't ask.

8. You must exceed your customer's expectations to effect maximum synergy relationships.

9. You must open your eyes wider to see the synergy opportunities around you.

10. Life is more than just showing up—life is what you do when you get there.

11. Insanity is repeating the same process and expecting a different result.

We have summarized these concepts during our conclusion because we do not feel that you can implement all the ideas you will have garnered from every aspect of synergy we have discussed. Trying to do that would just add more stress to your life. We are hoping you can choose one or two ideas and implement these in an orderly fashion. Do not change what you are already doing—just integrate a few synergy ideas into your present activities.

This summary is designed to help you transition from the "thinking" to the "choosing" process. Hopefully you have been thinking of areas for improvement throughout this book. But beware—if you choose too many activities you will just increase your levels of stress and not accomplish any improvements. You must focus your limited resources upon the one, two or three areas where you can achieve the most results. Even your implementation of the synergy rules must be organized with synergy in mind.

In this way we will start improving and adding productivity while minimizing the stress in our lives. There is no doubt about the fact that we are all facing an era that puts a premium on effecting more in less time. Unless we make adjustments that enable us to integrate this additional production without working twice as much, we will be stuck on the proverbial treadmill of life. With technology advancing, the treadmill will be moving faster and faster each year. Have you ever tried to get off a treadmill moving at full speed?

Only you can decide what actions you will take after learning about our maximum synergy rules. Whether you are in sales, operations, management or all three (this means you are a small business owner) everyone can benefit from achieving more with less resources. Does anyone seem to have spare time or money these days?

We think not. Good luck!

INDEX